LIFE IS GOOD!

"building success through optimism"

ROB McCARTER

ISBN Number 1-57087-417-4

Professional Press
Chapel Hill, NC 27515-4371

Manufactured in the United States of America
   00 01 02 03   10 9 8 7 6 5 4 3

DEDICATION

I respectfully dedicate this book to my parents,
Mr. & Ms. Robert C. McCarter Sr.

Acknowledgments

Having completed my third book, I realize more than ever the importance of the support of family and friends. Many thanks are given to the following:

My family:

> Ms. Selena McCarter, Mr. Jordan McCarter & Mr. Lawson McCarter...my family who support my dreams and visions

My CMS family who spent hours editing this manuscript:

> Ms. Barbara Hendrix
> Ms. Jil Hicks
> Mr. Bob Kleinschrod
> Ms. Laurie Knapp

To Ms. Brenda McCraw & Ms. Judy Marett...two wonderful ladies who have always believed in and supported my work.

To Ms. Nan Stines Clark, who in 1975, wrote these words in my yearbook, "You're a singer, a poet and a rascal, but I love the combination...and I think you'll be a success because you've got that secret happiness that draws people and radiates to everyone."

Contents

PRECONSTRUCTION ABOUT SUCCESS

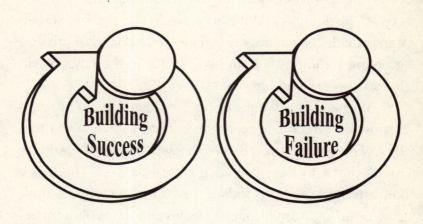

Does the name Navin Johnson sound familiar to you? Probably not, as he is not one of the more famous Johnsons (e.g., Lyndon, Howard, Don, or Ben). However, if you are a fan of the actor Steve Martin, then you might recognize the name as a character he played in the movie, "The Jerk." The movie chronicles a short period in the life of Navin Johnson. As the movie begins, we find Navin, unsophisticated in worldly ways and somewhat dimwitted, living the life of a drunk on the streets of Cityville, USA. As with many homeless individuals, overwhelmingly negative circumstances led to this lifestyle. As Navin begins to tell his story, we find that several months prior he lived in a small shack with his family in Ruralville, USA. The family was poor but for what they lacked in material wealth they made up for in love, devotion and care. They were happy. They were successful. Navin, upon discovering he was different from his family (e.g., he is European-American, they are African-American), decided to move to Cityville, USA, to "discover" his identity. With only the magic the big screen can provide, Navin arrives in Cityville and lands a job as a gasoline station attendant his first day in the city. Navin found success and happiness.

Within a few weeks of his employment, an incident happened which changed Navin's life forever. On that day Navin altered a customer's eyewear by soldering a metal brace to the nosepiece of his glasses. The brace kept the glasses from sliding down the customer's nose and/or falling from his face. His invention revolutionized the eyewear business. Eyeglass wearers everywhere bought Navin's invention. The end result, Navin became a millionaire; he had the mansion, the servants, the cars, the toys and the woman of his dreams. Life was good!

Perhaps too good. Just as quickly as Navin became wealthy, he became penniless. You see, there was an unanticipated side effect to his invention. The eyewear brace somehow caused the wearer to become cross-eyed. Refunds and lawsuits tapped into Navin's fortune; soon he was broke. He had lost it all-the mansion, the servants, the cars, the toys and the woman of his dreams. What a roller coaster ride! Within a few months, Navin's ride had gone from the heights of high society to the depths of a drunk on the streets.

Do not feel sorry for Navin. As is typical of movieland, Navin's story has a happy ending. Upon hearing of his plight, his family and the girl of his dreams searched Cityville until they found him. Literally, picking him up from the gutter they took him back to Ruralville where they loved and nurtured him. Life was good, again. As the movie ends, we are left to believe that Navin lived happily ever after.

This movie is intended to be humorous and entertaining, and it is. While it is not a serious movie, there are several inaccurate implied messages (probably unintended) which can distort the movie viewer's perception of success. Had this movie been the only one which contains these messages, I would not be concerned. Unfortunately, many movies and television programs contain similar messages. The more these messages are subconsciously fed into our minds, the more we believe them and the less successful we will be.

INACCURATE IMPLIED MESSAGE #1
POSSESSIONS VALIDATE SUCCESS

The first implication is that possessions validate success. In other words, the one with the most toys is the winner. The tragedy in this message lies in the fact that the "winner" soon discovers that what was won was not what had been anticipated. Material possessions alone do not give them the "happily ever after" life as described in fairy tales. The "winner" soon realizes that as the newness of each toy wears off, so does the feelings of success. As such, the "winners" begin to accumulate possession after possession after possession in hopes of recapturing those feelings. This never works! The one with the most toys is not, necessarily, the most successful.

In the movie, Navin was happy in Ruralville, USA with things that money couldn't buy (family, love, et cetera). He was also happy in Cityville, USA when he accumulated great wealth and things that money could buy. However, when he lost the wealth, he lost his happiness. That's because he redefined happiness and success in terms of material possessions instead of in terms of things money can't buy (family, love, et cetera). Had he not done this, he would have been better able to constructively cope with financial loss.

Don't misunderstand me, I am not suggesting the pursuit of possessions and wealth be avoided. Amenities of life make living easier. What I am suggesting is that success is more than financial prosperity and toys. One who is truly successful has found a delicate balance between prosperity, peace of mind and physical health. This is the "*total package of success*." Wouldn't it be tragic to reach all of your financial goals only to lose your peace of mind (e.g., depression, mental illness) and/or physical health in the process?

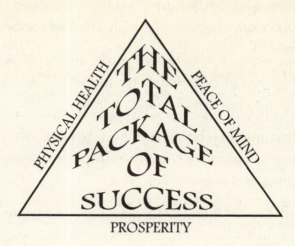

INACCURATE IMPLIED MESSAGE #2
SUCCESS CAN BE OBTAINED OVERNIGHT

A second implication lies in the message that success can be obtained overnight. Truthfully, sometimes it can, but more often it can not. History has provided us with unlimited examples of individuals who became successful in their respective fields. Ironically, most of them did not achieve success overnight. Instead, they overcame many obstacles and challenges as they struggled to achieve the total package of success. They are individuals who deliberately blueprinted their lives for unlimited success. Let's take a look at some life stories.

◆ Lucille Ball worked as a hat girl and waitress in New York for 22 years before landing her first major acting role.

- Colonel Harlan Sanders, a retiree, knocked on 1,009 doors before selling his chicken recipe.

- Alex Haley spent twelve years and was over $100,000 in debt when he found a publisher willing to publish his book, *Roots.*

- Winston Churchill's school life was filled with reports that stated, "no ambition, poor academic work and disruptive behavior."

- Rod Carew learned to play baseball using a broomstick for a bat, a tennis ball for a baseball and a paper bag for a glove.

- Walt Disney was told by a Kansas City news editor that his sketches showed no talent.

- Thomas Edison tried over 10,000 times to invent the light bulb before he was successful.

- Dolly Parton was the fourth of twelve children, living in a two-room wooden shack...she described her family as the poorest of all hillbillies.

- Albert Einstein exhibited significant problems in school because of difficulties in verbal skills...he was four years old before he could speak...one of this teachers stated, "He'll never amount to anything."

What can we learn from these examples of success in relation to the life of Navin Johnson? Primarily, that

Navin's story of success is the exception, not the rule. People want to believe that if they put forth a little effort, then rewards will come. Instant gratification is their theme and their work ethic reflects this. The result...when gratification does not come quickly and obstacles rise as they build for success, they quit. Their rationale is, "This success stuff is for the birds anyway." Success cannot be achieved overnight. It must be a daily construction process that is built by the thoughts you think throughout life. This is the more rational message.

INACCURATE IMPLIED MESSAGE #3
THE LAW OF FINANCIAL EQUILIBRIUM

A third implication involves the belief that, "Good times never last." "The Jerk" leaves us with the impression that those financially challenged cannot achieve lasting financial success because something or someone "out there" is going to take it. Lasting financial success is too good to be true. To believe this is to believe in the law of financial equilibrium in which the rich get richer and the poor get poorer.

Is there a law of financial equilibrium which must be maintained? I do not think so. Two of the benefits which should accompany financial success are the right to enjoy success and to confidently believe in your ability to maintain and increase it.

On the other hand, if you believe in the law of financial equilibrium, what do you think will result from new found financial success? You will not be able to fully enjoy your success as you are constantly expecting circumstances beyond your control to once again leave you without financial prosperity. Not a desirable way to live, is it?

Message Mania

How many movies and television programs have you viewed which tend to contain one or more of these messages? The number could be in the hundreds or thousands. It has been well documented the effect that movies and television programs have on the proliferation of violence. Couldn't a similar phenomena be occurring in which the viewer, because of inaccurate implied messages, is subconsciously inhibited from lasting and true success? I think so.

Just Have To

One of my favorite avocations involves coaching Little League baseball. I "just have to" coach. Each spring, as I begin to prepare myself for this avocation, I remind myself that I must accept the responsibility for transforming a group of youngsters with varying skills and goals into a team which maximizes their skills to achieve a common goal. The tools of my trade include inspiring, teaching, motivating, disciplining and nurturing. The degree and extent to which I am successful determines the success of the team.

Likewise, my goal in writing this book is to serve as your coach for success. It is my responsibility to accept you at your present success skill level and to help you increase your level as much as you desire. In this book you will be inspired, taught, motivated, disciplined and nurtured into maximizing your potential.

CHANGE IS POSSIBLE!

The good news is that change is possible. I have changed; so can you. In this book you will learn how. Step by step you'll be directed and coached into building unlimited success. You will find a simple and to-the-point writing approach designed to facilitate change as soon as possible.

Now is the time to put on your uniform, strap on your cleats and join the team of those who experience unlimited success. Unlimited success will increase within your internal world (i.e., mind) and then in your external world as you:

♦ develop a blueprint which shouts to the world, "Life is good!"

♦ lay a foundation of "mind over matter"

♦ frame your mind with constructive thoughts

♦ plumb (cleanse) your mind by increasing your IQ

♦ electrify your life with ACTION

◆ replace complacency with constant maintenance

Phase I
Developing A Blueprint For Success

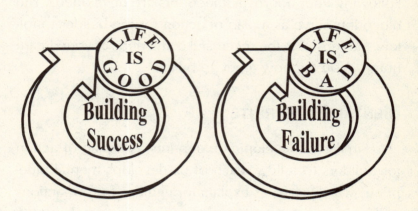

Pretend that you just won a million dollars in a sweepstakes! The sole requirement for claiming the prize is that you must spend the entire amount in building your dream home. How would you proceed to build? Would you develop a building plan which included the random selection of building materials joined together in a haphazard fashion by inexperienced laborers? This would not likely be your plan of action. Haphazard chaotic planning would soon consume the building process resulting in a "scream" home not a dream home.

Chances are you would choose a more systematic plan from which to build your home. A plan which assured quality, durability, character and pride. To accomplish this goal you would likely spend hours in meetings with a knowledgeable and competent architect. During these meetings, you share ideas and pictures of your dream home. The architect in turn transfers your ideas to paper by sketching visual representations of your future home. Following your approval, blueprints are developed. The blueprints serve as a plan of action for the builder to follow, thus ensuring the successful completion of your dream home. You are now ready to build.

Mental Blueprints

Similar to developing blueprints as a plan of action for builders to follow, each of us develops mental blueprints, which serve as explanatory guides for our actions and feelings in a given situation. There are two characteristics in everyone's mental blueprints that make them a powerful force in their lives.

The first characteristic of a mental blueprint is that it is learned. Learning which results from a funneling process. Let's use an analogy to clarify. When I was a child, I was the neighborhood grass-cutter. It was a good paying job with a window view. As my business grew, my parents informed me that if I planned to stay in business, I needed to perform routine maintenance on the lawn mower. This included checking and maintaining an acceptable oil level in the motor. The first couple of times I attempted to add oil, I spilled more on the chassis than I poured into the mower. My profits were diminishing by the minute. Out of necessity, I thought of investing some of my profits in a funnel...a plastic object designed with a large opening on one end and a small opening on the other. Its main function is to allow the user to put fluid into the large end which then drains to the small end and goes into whatever small hole it was designed to fill. I used it to fill my lawn mower with oil.

While contemplating the ways and means in which our mental blueprints develop, I began to think of the funneling process. Our mental blueprints do not suddenly come to us. They are learned and developed as the result of many influences in our lives. Influences from family, friends, media, socioeconomic class, religious upbringing,

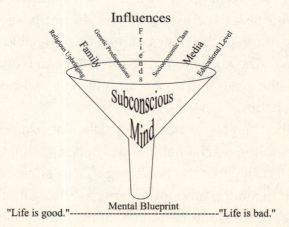

Influences

Subconscious Mind

Mental Blueprint

"Life is good."---"Life is bad."

educational level and genetic predisposition are combined and classified within the body of the funnel (i.e., the subconscious mind) until the result is a learned habitual way of thinking. The funneling process is complete around the age of eight. From this point forward, these influences work together to form a blueprint for success or a blueprint for failure. Success occurs when our blueprints primarily reflect that "Life is good," while failure occurs when our blueprints primarily reflect that "Life is bad."

The second powerful characteristic of one's mental blueprint lies in its habitual nature. Think with me for a moment about the power that physical habits have over people. Habits are actions which automatically occur in specific situations. Some habits are beneficial because they improve the quality of our lives (e.g., brushing our teeth, exercising). Others are beneficial because they keep us from "reinventing the wheel" each time we want to perform a task. For example, you do not have to consciously return to the basics of reading to be able to read this book. The ability to recognize letters, to blend them, to scan the page and so on are efficient and necessary reading habits.

Other habits are not beneficial. For example, one familiar nonbeneficial habit is the action of biting one's nails. It is likely that this habit begins as a stress reaction. Over an extended amount of time, as stressful situations increase, so does the frequency of nail biting. Soon nail biting becomes habitual with a seemingly "life of its own."

Likewise, our mental blueprints are habitual. Once they are learned, they become the automatic way we view most, if not all, circumstances of life. Our success or failure in life is a direct reflection of our learned habitual mental blueprint.

MENTAL BLUEPRINT CONTINUUM

Just as life is not an absolute, neither are mental blueprints. NO one believes that "life is good" all of the time just as NO one believes "life is bad" all of the time. In actuality the two beliefs are endpoints on a continuum. As such, everyone's mental blueprint can be plotted at some point between the two absolute endpoints.

The more strongly one believes "life is good," the more optimistic they will be. When faced with a problem, they will actively seek to solve it, or at the very least, manage it. They are adept at rising above the negative circumstance. Unlimited success is theirs as they enjoy the fruits of their efforts.

Conversely, the more strongly one believes that "life is bad," the more pessimistic they will be. When faced with a problem, they will view it as unmanageable and overwhelming. Many times you'll find them under the negative circumstance. Limited success is theirs because of their inability to enjoy the fruits of their efforts.

Which mental blueprint do you think would be more conducive to:

- High achievement?
- Mental health?
- Physical health?

The answer is obvious; it's the optimistic mental blue-print. Lest you misunderstand, this statement is not an illusion. It's not psychobabble. An optimistic mental blue-print has proven benefits. A vast number of research studies into the phenomena of optimistic thinking have led to three primary categories of benefits.

Benefit #1: High Achievers

People who are optimistic thinkers have been found to be high achievers. Achievement has been studied in a variety of areas (e.g., college students, insurance sales, and professional sports such as baseball and basketball). For example, in 1993 I conducted a study that examined the role optimistic mental blueprints play in the success (e.g., wins and losses) of a professional basketball team. Since a person's unrehearsed remarks often are a reflection of their blueprint, I analyzed individual player's comments following games (both wins and losses).

The results were not unexpected. First, the extent to which any player was optimistic (i.e., "life is good") or pessimistic (i.e., "life is bad") determined their ability to recover from the effects of a loss. Secondly, their mental blueprint determined their ability to build upon a win for greater success in the future. Optimistic thinking allowed them to maximize their talent.

Likewise, optimistic thinking will allow you to maximize your talent for success, not vice versa. Many people believe that talent allows them to maximize their success.

By the very definition of "talent" this logically cannot be true. Talent is defined as an innate mental or artistic ability less than genius. That means that two percent of the population (i.e., genius group) is immediately excluded because of superior skills and abilities. Conversely, another two percent have to be excluded from being talented because of inferior skills and abilities (i.e., mentally handicapped group). Single digit addition will tell you that the product of the two groups equals four percent.

McCarter's Math
2+2=96
"What's Your Excuse?"

2% ←——————— 96% ———————→ 2%

Talent Scale

What does this say about the rest of us? It says that ninety-six percent of us have the raw materials (e.g., mental capacity) necessary to fulfill the criteria of talented. In other words, we are talented!

If we are talented, then why aren't we successful? Because talent will not drive you to maximize your potential. Talent is not the internal force that pushes us to pick ourselves up off the mat for another round when the circumstances of life knock us down. It does not give us the persistence, confidence and desire that is evident in the lives of high achievers. While talent is an important factor in one's ability to achieve, it is merely a complimentary player.

The main player is one's mental blueprint. Research shows that those who express an optimistic mental blueprint are not defeated psychologically by adversity in their lives. Instead, they view the adversity as a hurdle to overcome, as merely a temporary roadblock to who they are and where they want to go. Thus, they are willing to do what it takes to overcome the adversity or until they, through trial and effort, come to the conclusion that they have done everything possible to alleviate the adversity. In either case, a sense of satisfaction is obtained from giving forth their best effort.

Benefit #2: Physical Health

For years, the relationship between the mind and the body has been studied by a number of professional disciplines. Former Surgeon General C. Everett Koop, said that over 90% of all health related problems have a cognitive component. In other words, many times it's the negative things that we dwell on that result in physical problems for our bodies. This has been the conjecture of physicians for decades. Dr. John Schindler, in his book, *How To Live 365 Days A Year*, stated that most of the common physical symptoms displayed by his patients were not physiologically but psychologically based as a result of stress.

SCHINDLER'S LIST

SYMPTOM	PERCENTAGE-STRESS RELATED
Pain in Back of Neck	75%
Lump in Throat	90%
Ulcer-Like Pain	50%
Gall Bladder-Like Pain	50%
Gas	99.44%
Dizziness	80%
Headaches	80%
Constipation	70%
Tiredness	90%

Stress is perhaps the main byproduct of a pessimistic mental blueprint. The phenomenon of stress dates to pre-historic times. Cavemen were frequently in situations where they either had to prepare to fight the adversity (e.g., saber-tooth tiger, fellow caveman) or flee from it. A physiological response was inherent in their bodies that assisted them in whatever action they deemed necessary.

The same physiological response occurs within our bodies today. We are "pre-wired" to react chemically whenever we face a perceived stressor. Thus, the body is prepared for action (to either fight or flee). In our society, the options to fight or flee from our stressors are seldom appropriate options. Therefore, instead of actively dissipating the chemical reaction within our body, we internalize it. Internalization, without action, will result in physiological symptoms similar to that Schindler has described. Eventually the body will break down; a breakdown that began with a "life is bad" mental blueprint.

How do we gain control of these stressors? We must take away the situation's power by maintaining a "life is good" mental blueprint, thus effectively stopping the chemical reaction that is so dangerous to our physical health.

Not only will an optimistic mental blueprint diminish the effects of stress in our lives, but one who believes that "life is good," will live a lifestyle that promotes wellness. They are aware of the effects of an unhealthy lifestyle. For example, optimistic thinkers are more likely to exercise and eat nutritious foods while simultaneously minimizing the use of alcohol and tobacco. By doing these things, they lessen the odds of contracting major illnesses as they avoid many of the causal agents (e.g., fatty foods, alcohol, tobacco, sedentary lifestyle) for diseases.

Note, I said an optimistic mental blueprint lessens the odds of illnesses, this doesn't mean they eliminate the odds. Optimistic thinkers also get sick. However, the benefits to optimistic thinkers lie in two areas. First, they tend to get sick less often due to their healthy lifestyle and a strong immune system. Secondly, once they do get sick they recover more quickly.

BENEFIT #3: MENTAL HEALTH

People who are optimistic thinkers are less likely to allow the negative events in their lives to result in mental difficulties...primarily depression. Depression is so common in our society that it is known as the "common cold" of mental health. The results of depression can be devastating. The ability to effectively eliminate depression in one's life is important for at least two reasons.

The first reason involves the risk of suicide. Not all people who attempt suicide are depressed, but of those who attempt suicide, approximately 85% were initially depressed. Optimistic thinking tends to counter this phenomenon. When adversity strikes, optimistic thinkers do not engage in destructive self-talk which results from mutilations (e.g., "it's all my fault"), mountainations (e.g., "it's awful") and/or musterbations (e.g., "things must be perfect"). Destructive self-talk such as this leads to hopelessness, a major characteristic of depression. Depressed people have lost hope for a better day.

The second reason to eliminate depression involves the byproducts of depression. Since depressed people tend to withdraw, function at a minimum, be inner focused, and give up easily, their lifestyle touches the lives of those around them. Those around them experience an emotional roller coaster as they watch their loved one suffer.

PERSONAL TESTIMONY

Wouldn't it be a shame to reach all of your achievement goals (the American dream) and yet not be mentally or physically healthy enough to enjoy them? It happens. Many have chased the American dream only to lose other aspects of their lives (e.g., family, and health) in the process. I know from a personal perspective no one is immune.

At the age of twenty-three, I was married to the woman of my dreams and gainfully employed as a school psychologist. I was financially prospering. I imagine that to most people, I had it made; yet I was miserable. It showed in my emotions (anger, stress) and in my physical health (e.g., high blood pressure, weight gain). I was self-destructing. I knew that life had to be better than this. Using my psychological training, I soon discovered that the root of all my conflict lay in my blueprint for life. To me, "life was bad." To rewrite an entrenched blueprint is hard work, but I did it (and am doing it everyday). The teachings I used to rewrite my blueprint are included in this book. They work!

Before you misinterpret my point, I'm not saying that optimistic thinking is the "answer" to all of human misery and suffering; this is not the case. An optimistic thinking lifestyle is not a panacea. You will still have problems and challenges to meet, manage and solve. With optimistic thinking skills, however, you can meet and respond to these challenges more effectively.

THE GOOD NEWS

The good news lies in the fact that, while you may have developed your blueprint based on past influences, it is changeable. You *learned* to think as you do! That means if you are not happy with "where" you are in life, you can rewrite your mental blueprint. Let me say this again,

YOU CAN REWRITE YOUR MENTAL BLUEPRINT!

This news alone is an awesome revelation. This means that there is hope for everyone. If you have developed a "life is bad" mental blueprint and are unhappy with the results you are getting from it, you can develop a new mental blueprint...a blueprint which shouts to the world, "LIFE IS GOOD!"

WHO NEEDS TO THINK OPTIMISTICALLY?

Who needs to think optimistically? Everyone! Especially those whose lives and/or professions include a high potential for failure and frustration. That includes all of us. Those of us who have blueprinted our lives with optimistic thinking will reap the benefits.

SUCCESS POINT

TO BUILD FOR SUCCESS, DEVELOP A BLUEPRINT WHICH SHOUTS TO THE WORLD, "LIFE IS GOOD!"

PHASE II
LAYING A FOUNDATION FOR SUCCESS

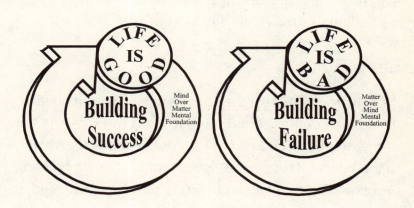

To reiterate from phase I, everyone has learned a habitual way of explaining circumstances in their lives. This is called a mental blueprint. Their mental blueprint determines everything they do, say and feel. For example, if their mental blueprint reflects optimism (i.e., "Life is good!") they will be mentally prepared to experience more of the *total package of success* (i.e., prosperity, physical health, peace of mind). On the other hand, if their mental blueprint reflects pessimism (i.e., "Life is bad.") they will not be mentally prepared to experience the *total package of success* in all its fullness.

The good news is that anyone can experience the *total package of success* that an optimistic blueprint provides. However, it takes a conscious effort to build and maintain it. A building and maintaining process which is analogous to the building of a home. Aren't our bodies, in a sense, our home? The only way to build either home is from the ground up. If standards are not met or exceeded, then success will not occur.

Let's Build

The foundation of the home is mostly buried beneath the surface of the ground. As such, it is rarely a concern of the homeowner...out of sight, out of mind. However, to the builder it is the most important part of the building process. The builder's concern is based on knowledge that dates back as far as Biblical times when men were encouraged to build houses upon rocky ground and not upon sandy ground. The reasoning for this was, as it still is, very simple...a sandy foundation does not provide the home with the underlying strength and support necessary to withstand the forces of nature. Regardless of the home's uniqueness and beauty, a home built upon a sandy foundation will soon tilt, crumble and fall. Consequently, the builder digs and digs and digs into the ground until he finds a rock-solid place upon which to lay a foundation.

MENTAL FOUNDATIONS

Likewise, if we are to build for success we must dig and dig and dig into mental ground until we find a rock solid mental surface upon which to lay a foundation. Without a rock solid mental foundation, when the negative forces come (e.g., obstacles, problems, and challenges) to block our success we will tilt, crumble or fall...we will be unable to maintain our uniqueness and beauty.

Just as there are two types of building foundations, there are two types of mental foundations. The one we base our lives on is directly proportionate to the degree that we succeed or fail.

MATTER OVER MIND MENTAL FOUNDATION

The first basic mental foundation is one of "matter over mind." Essentially a "matter over mind" thinker operates from the belief that because it matters they mind. The "it" is the particular circumstance which contributed to the problem that is blocking success. As such, whenever a problem occurs the solution is to change the "it" in hopes of eliminating the problem, thus achieving success in a particular area.

A surface (above ground) inspection of this problem solving approach leads one to conclude that matter over mind is a rock solid foundation upon which to build for success. It's only when one inspects under the surface that one begins to see the flaws (sandy base) in such an approach. Flaws which are inherent in each step of the problem solving process.

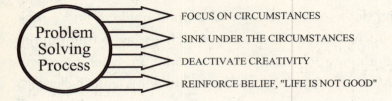

FOCUS ON CIRCUMSTANCES

SINK UNDER THE CIRCUMSTANCES

DEACTIVATE CREATIVITY

REINFORCE BELIEF, "LIFE IS NOT GOOD"

⇨ FOCUS ON CIRCUMSTANCE

As the above illustration portrays, when a problem arises immediate and undivided attention and energy is expended on the precipitating circumstance(s). In truth, often times initial success occurs when one focuses on changing the circumstances. However, success is rarely permanent because of other uncontrollable and unforeseen factors which contributed to the problem. The inability to control these factors dampens enthusiasm and motivation; soon failure replaces success.

⇨ SINK UNDER THE CIRCUMSTANCE

To compensate, the individual reacts with a more intense focus and energy on the precipitating circumstance, or shift their attention to another perceived precipitating circumstance. The failure pattern is repeated.

Repeated failure leads to hopelessness and a belief they are "sinking under the circumstances." One who is sinking under the circumstances is easy to identify. This is the individual who answers your rhetorical question "How are you doing?" with the reply, "I'm doing OK under the circumstances." When I get that reply, I immediately visualize the person as shouldering a large bag of negative circumstances while standing in quicksand which is rising over their head.

The more they sink and struggle against the load, the more hopeless they feel. In order to regain their hope, they begin to display magical thinking for circumstantial change. They get caught up in, "WHEN I; THEN I" magical thinking. Comments you may hear from someone sinking under the circumstances are:

"*When I* win the sweepstakes; *then I* will be successful."

"*When I* get a new house (or car, or boat, or, or, or); *then I* will be happy."

"*When I* get a new job; then *I will* be successful."

⇨ **DEACTIVATE CREATIVITY**

The more they sink and the more they "WHEN I; THEN I," the less likely they will be able to creatively solve their problems. Their ability to solve problems in new or unexpected ways will be nonexistent. Instead of looking for creative ways to succeed, they are subconsciously looking for ways to fail.

⇨ REINFORCES BELIEF, "LIFE IS NOT GOOD"

With all hope gone, their lives begin to tilt, crumble and fall. Failure overrides success potential. Their mental foundation has led them through a problem solving approach, which reinforced their belief that "Life is bad!"

Sandy-Shallow

An inspection of a "matter over mind" mental foundation leads one to conclude that it is based on a sandy and shallow foundation. Those who have laid this foundation simply have not dug deep enough to be able to effectively solve problems and to lead successful lives. I have witnessed the evidence of this many times in counseling sessions with high school students. Many who have sought my counsel have done so as a final desperate means of relief from a problem; a problem which they have repeatedly failed to solve. Once we get past the "matter over mind" mental foundation, we are able to lay a new foundation and problems can be solved.

However, we should not judge their initial lack of success as a sign of the inexperience of youth. In truth, it's not. Circumstantial focus is a typical problem solving strategy used across all age groups. For many, it's entrenched in their belief system...a belief system which subconsciously leads to actions and feelings as written in the "Pessimist Creed."

PESSIMIST CREED

Promise Yourself

To be so weak that everything disturbs your peace of mind.

To talk sickness, sadness, and poverty to every person you meet.

To make all your friends feel that there is nothing in them.

To look at the dark side of everything and make your pessimism come true.

To think only of the worst, to work only for the worst and to expect only the worst.

To be jealous of the success of others.

To remember the mistakes of the past and live on previous achievements of days gone by.

To wear a frown at all times and give every living creature you meet a frown.

To give so little time to the improvement of yourself that all you do is criticize others.

To worry all of the time, easily lose your temper, be constantly fearful and so unhappy that you welcome trouble.

Mind over Matter

The second basic mental foundation is one of "mind over matter." Those who have laid this mental foundation would agree wholeheartedly with Marx (Groucho not Karl) who said the best way to face negative circumstance is with "mind over matter." More specifically he said, "if you don't mind, then it don't matter." What Groucho intended as a joke has some significant success building implications. For instance, instead of focusing on the role of precipitating circumstances (i.e., "it"), focus on the role the mind (beliefs, thoughts) plays in solving the problem. Those who have laid a "mind over matter" mental foundation believe that the solution to the problem lies more within their mind (belief) than in changing the circumstance. As such, whenever a success-blocking problem occurs, they look inward (as opposed to outward) for solutions. By doing so, they've aligned themselves with some of the greatest thinkers and achievers of all time.

One such great thinker with whom I've aligned myself with is Jesus Christ. Throughout Christ's short ministry on earth he taught about the importance of faith (belief) as the number one factor to overcoming problems. Time and time again He demonstrated that when we act on our beliefs, solutions occur. On one occasion there was a woman who went to Him for healing of an affliction. Despite the large crowd surrounding Jesus, the woman somehow was able to get close enough to him to touch the hem of His garment. Upon touching Jesus, her belief was rewarded as she was immediately healed.

What do you think would have happened had the woman succumbed to the seemingly overwhelming circumstances (e.g., her affliction, and large crowd around Jesus)? She would have died from her affliction.

Another one whom I consider to be a great thinker was the first century Greek philosopher named Epictetus. Epictetus was a freed slave who dedicated his life to the teaching of Stoicism, a philosophy that emphasizes morality and tolerance for others. Based upon his observations, he determined that, "Man is disturbed NOT by things but by the views he takes of them."

What do you think would have happened had Epictetus used a past life of slavery as an excuse not to learn the secrets of successful living and to teach them to others? He would have been one of the countless others who have walked the earth living a mediocre life.

Epictetus and Jesus Christ are but two who laid a mental foundation of "mind over matter." However, despite their successes a foundation inspection is warranted before we can conclude it is a rock solid foundation for solving problems and for building for success.

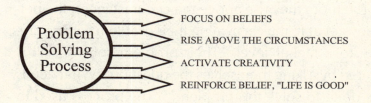

Problem Solving Process

FOCUS ON BELIEFS

RISE ABOVE THE CIRCUMSTANCES

ACTIVATE CREATIVITY

REINFORCE BELIEF, "LIFE IS GOOD"

⇨ **FOCUS ON BELIEFS**

As the above illustration portrays, when a problem arises immediate and undivided attention is focused on the solution. It's not that circumstances are ignored, it's that the "mind over matter" person realizes that it's almost impossible to find a solution while focusing on the success-blocking circumstance. They believe and act on their mental capacity to find a solution.

⇨ **RISE ABOVE THE CIRCUMSTANCES**

That is not to say that the "mind over matter" person is immune to the negative effects of problems. On the contrary, when problems occur they also tilt, crumble and sometimes fall. Yet amazingly, the more they look past the circumstances, the more they find themselves repairing the damage done by the circumstances and rising above them. The actor Christopher Reeve is one such example...despite being a quadriplegic from an accident, he has continued to work in the entertainment field as both an actor and a director.

⇨ **ACTIVATE CREATIVITY**

The more they rise above the circumstances, the better they get at it, thus activating their problem solving creativity to a higher level. Their problem solving skill is activated by asking themselves the question, "What needs to be done to solve this problem?" The process used to obtain the solution is just as important as the solution it-self, for it is a process which can be used time after time to stimulate creativity to find solutions.

One successful process was one I discussed in my last book, *Optimistic Thinking: The Key To Success.* In the book, I introduced the "Possibility Thinking Game." Due to its popularity, I shall repeat it here.

POSSIBILITY THINKING GAME

1. What problem am I currently facing? (be as specific and objective as possible)

2. What strategies can I use to meet this problem? (brainstorm and list 10 ways the problem can be solved)

3. What next? (implement your strategy)

4. Did it work? (if no, modify the strategy, choose another strategy, or *manage* the problem

⇨ REINFORCE BELIEF, "LIFE IS GOOD"

"The Possibility Thinking Game" is an effective tool for obtaining solutions. However, there will be times when despite your best efforts, solutions will not come. During those times you can use a similar process by asking yourself, "How can I manage this problem?" From that point, develop strategies which will help you manage it.

Regardless of whether the problem is managed or solved, the person's mental blueprint, "Life is good," is still intact because they can rest in the assurance they did everything they knew to do to meet the challenge head on. They used their mind to overcome the negative matters in their lives.

ROCK-SOLID

An inspection of the "mind over matter" mental foundation leads one to conclude that it is based on a rock-solid foundation. Those who have laid this foundation simply have dug and dug and dug until they learned to solve problems by putting mind over matter. Just as I have observed many who in counseling sessions had laid a foundation of "matter over mind," I have been privileged to personally know many successful people who have built for success by laying a foundation of "mind over matter."

Perhaps those most important to me are my parents. Bob & Barbara McCarter were reared in families of 15 and 10 brothers and sisters respectively. You can imagine the economic strain on each family. To help support their respective families, they each quit school in the tenth grade. However, my parents didn't allow the circumstance to dictate their economic future for themselves or their children. Both served as role models for me as to the importance of education when they earned their high school equivalencies and college degrees.

A second example is a man by the name of Duane Reid. Duane was the youngest of nine children with all the children sharing one bedroom of a four-room house. The neighborhood he grew up in contained bootlegged liquor and drug houses. The potential for violence and failure was all around him. Despite the potentially adverse environment, Duane learned from his parents the importance of preparing yourself to succeed. Reid learned those lessons well as now he has beaten the odds by becoming the owner of two successful Ford dealerships in South Carolina.

The last example of the power of mind over matter is a woman by the name of Susan Cloninger. As an infant, Susan was diagnosed with spinal muscular atrophy. However, her parents taught her that she could accomplish anything if she tried hard enough. As such, she chose to overcome the disability and has succeeded through determination and optimism. Today, Cloninger's life is full as she cares for a husband and daughter, works full time, lectures to groups regarding the architectural and societal barriers that a handicapped person faces and is Ms. Wheelchair North Carolina.

The McCarters, Reid and Cloninger represent but three of the countless number of nonfamous people who utilize a "mind over matter" approach to succeed in life. They are active success builders. In addition, I'm sure they would readily concur that the pursuit of success is a tough pursuit and that anyone who actively builds for success will encounter more problems and challenges than the one building for failure. That's because it's easier to build a mediocre or average life than to be successful.

However, for those who seek to overcome the average and mediocre life, the rewards are endless. For success builders, a mind over matter approach is entrenched in their belief system...a belief system which unconsciously leads to actions and feelings as written in the "Optimist Creed."

Optimist Creed

Promise Yourself

To be so strong that nothing can disturb your
peace of mind.

To talk health, happiness and prosperity to
every person you meet.

To make all your friends feel that there is
something in them.

To look at the sunny side of everything
and make your optimism come true.

To think only of the best, to work only for the best and
expect only the best.

To be just as enthusiastic about the success of others as you are about your own.

To forget the mistakes of the past and press on to the greater achievements of the future.

To wear a cheerful countenance at all times and give every living creature you meet a smile.

To give so much time to the improvement of yourself that you have no time to criticize others.

To be too large for worry, too noble for anger, too strong for fear and too happy to permit the presence of trouble.

There is a difference...

There is a difference between the mental foundations of "mind over matter" versus "matter over mind." The end does indeed justify the means as a "mind over matter" mental foundation will result in a "Life is good" blueprint. Likewise, the end result of a "matter over mind" mental foundation leads to a "Life is bad" blueprint.

The crux of a foundation for success can be summed up in three words,

MIND OVER MATTER!

These words are not intended to simplify a profound truth. The mental foundation for success (i.e., prosperity, physical health, and peace of mind) lies in our ability to understand that our beliefs, NOT the negative circumstances, should be used to overcome the storms of life.

CONSIDER THIS...

Despite information presented to the contrary, some reading this will still cling to the belief that it's the circumstances in their lives that cause failure. If you are one of these, then I beg you to honestly explain to me how:

♦ someone who faces similar circumstances as you has achieved prosperity, physical health and/or peace of mind

OR

♦ someone who faces worse circumstances than you has achieved prosperity, physical health and/or peace of mind

Both of these scenarios ask some tough and potent questions. Questions that require honest answers. As we have seen, the world is full of people who started out in, or are in, similar or worse circumstances than you and yet have the audacity to pass you in the prosperity, physical health and/or peace of mind departments. Perhaps you have concluded they are:

♦ more intelligent than you...they're not!

- more talented than you...they're not!

- luckier than you...they're not!

Or Maybe They're

- too stupid to realize how bad they have it...not so!

None of these conclusions are accurate. The truth is, this group of people are like you in that their foundation rocks when stormy weather (negative circumstances) hits. They, too, hurt, get discouraged and disappointed. The difference between them and you is they have found, maybe not through books, but from daily living, that they do not have to be slaves to their "lot" in life. They do not give credence to the myth that their situation determines their success. The mental foundation for them is not in what happens to them from the external world but what happens between their own ears; their interpretation of events. This is the first vital step in rewriting your blueprint for success.

SUCCESS POINT

TO BUILD FOR SUCCESS, LAY A FOUNDATION OF "MIND OVER MATTER"

PHASE III
FRAMING FOR SUCCESS

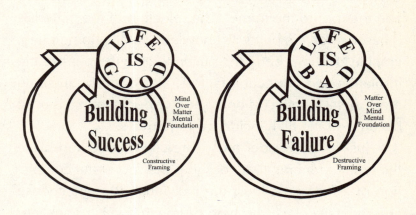

The message to us is clear. Just as a homebuilder must choose a rock solid piece of land upon which to lay a foundation, so must the success builder choose a rock-solid mental foundation upon which to build. Success builders utilize a "mind over matter" mental foundation.

Upon completion of the home's foundation, the builder confidently begins the third phase; namely, framing the structure. The framing phase of the building process is the seemingly complicated chore of intricately joining a system of studs, floor joists and rafters to form the shell of the home. A shell that serves two purposes.

The first purpose is as a support system. The frame of the home supports the wires and pipes, which carry electrical currents and water respectively. In addition, it also supports television cable and telephone wiring.

The second purpose is to protect and insulate the home from potential detrimental external and internal elements. This is accomplished by attaching floors, walls and the roof to the frame. The selection of the materials is based upon the builder's knowledge of the home's geographic location. Thus, the builder is able to optimize the insulation and protection factors. For example, in some areas metal framing (as opposed to wood framing) is used because of the high incidence of termites.

Just as the builder must carefully choose and place the type of framing that goes into the successful completion of a house, so must the individual carefully choose and mentally place the type of framing which goes into his or her success building.

Have you ever?

Have you ever heard someone describe another person as having a "terrible frame of mind?" If you have, you're already clued into the essence of phase III. While we all follow a blueprint that reflects our view of the world, this blueprint is supported by a conglomeration of individual thoughts. Thoughts which are used to frame our world, our reality. Each thought can be compared to a single stud, joist or rafter in a home. As these thoughts daily number in the thousands, they have a tremendous impact on our mental blueprints. If we frame our mental blueprints with constructive thoughts, our lives will reflect appropriate actions and feelings. Conversely, if we frame our mental blueprints with destructive thoughts, our lives will reflect inappropriate actions and feelings. This conglomeration of thoughts form framing types.

The key to successful framing lies in our ability to identify both destructive and constructive framing types. Many times we are not aware of the devastating effect that an individual destructive framing type has on our mental blueprint and, ultimately, our quality of life. The focus of this phase is to help us learn to identify the framing types that lead to a pessimistic mental blueprint.

This is not as difficult as it seems as identification occurs simply by listening to the words we say. After all, aren't our words a direct reflection of our thoughts?

DESTRUCTIVE FRAMING TYPE #1
MUTILATIONS

"What caused this?" This is perhaps one of the oldest and most frequently asked questions of all time. History has given us multiple examples of man's attempt to explain life by attributing "cause" or responsibility to his or others' deeds.

The quest for causality continues today. Disasters such as an airplane crash, a violent murder, or the death of a princess, prompt us to instantaneously ask, "Who (What) caused this?" Our internal response to this question determines the actions and feelings that follow.

If causality is necessary to find a solution then it's constructive, however more times than not the search for causality is destructive because it leads to unrealistic blame and does not lend itself to a solution. More specifically, thoughts become destructive when one *habitually* interprets the cause and blame of most (if not all) challenging situations to be due to either a personal flaw or to a flaw in someone or something else. I refer to people who think in this way as psychological mutilators. Psychological mutilators mentally cripple and maim themselves and others psychologically, much like physical mutilators physically cripple and maim themselves and others.

There are two types of mutilators. The first type is the self-mutilator. Self-mutilators automatically blame themselves whenever a hardship, problem or challenge arises. They reason that the problem would not have occurred if not for personal internal (e.g., lack of intelligence, bad temper) or external (e.g., height, weight, race, socioeconomic status, sex) flaws. Unfortunately, we find too many people in our society today who are self-mutilators. It's as if they are to blame for every problem in their lives or in the lives of those around them. Examples of self-mutilation are abundant. One example is the self-mutilating mother who incorrectly rationalizes that she is not a good parent because her child exhibits behavior problems at school. Another example is the person who incorrectly concludes he or she was omitted from a committee because they weren't smart enough, talented enough, or popular enough and so on.

What do you think the self-mutilating style of explaining circumstances does to you? It mentally cripples and maims you. The primary area of psychological crippling occurs to one's self-image. Our self-image is the mental picture we have of ourselves. It develops as we compare our strengths, weaknesses, competencies and inadequacies with others. Through comparisons, self-mutilators have concluded they do not compare favorably with others. They believe they are inferior. A belief which is maintained regardless of evidence to the contrary.

An unfortunate consequence of self-mutilation occurs in how others relate to the self-mutilator; because they see themselves as inferior, others will see them as such. Consequently, they are treated in like manner to other's images of them. The self-mutilator has created a "self-fulfilling prophecy." To see yourself as inferior and to have others relate to you as if you are inferior, worthless and incompetent, leads to victimization. Self-mutilators are victims in this world. When hardships and challenges arise, they either don't try, give up or react destructively. The self-mutilator concludes, "Life is not good."

The second type of mutilator is the person who accuses or blames someone or something else when hardships occur. They are called other-mutilators. Other-mutilators, through their inaccurate sense of superiority, focus on "finger-pointing" and persecuting.

The consequences of other-mutilating can be just as psychologically crippling as self-mutilating. For instance, finger-pointing, in the mind of the other-mutilator, absolves them from taking responsibility for the problem. They live by the creed, "It's hard to fly with the eagles when you're surrounded by turkeys." Consequently, when challenges arise, they respond with anger and refusal to participate in the solution-process. Other-mutilators are the "persecutors" of this world. To the other mutilator, "Life is not good."

DESTRUCTIVE FRAMING TYPE #2
MOUNTAINATIONS

Do you remember the childhood story of *Chicken Little*? One day as Chicken Little was walking through the barnyard, she was hit in the head by an apple which fell from a tree. Immediately, Chicken Little concluded the sky was falling. Her exaggeration of the circumstance led her into a state of fear, which translated to a panic-stricken race around the barnyard to warn the other animals that the sky was falling. Soon the entire barnyard was in chaos.

Chicken Little's conclusion and corresponding action is typical of many people today. How many of us when faced with a challenging situation immediately assess the severity of it by mentally asking, "How bad is it?" Our assessment of the situation determines our actions.

If severity seeking contributes to a successful solution or resolution, then it's constructive. However, more times than not, an assessment of severity is destructive because the panic and fear it produces blocks success.

Everyone has observed firsthand the effects that exaggerating can have in a person's life. Exaggerators are everywhere. We encounter them in all walks of life. Every office, church, school or family has at least one such individual. These are people who *habitually* interpret even the most insignificant difficulty as awful or terrible. As one old phrase so aptly hails, they "make mountains out of molehills." Mountains which begin to loom larger than life; mountains larger than Mt. Everest. Thus the framing type, "mountainations."

Habitual mountainating is destructive for two reasons. First, as previously mentioned, it creates fear in the person's life and in the lives of those around them. Fear can be defined as "false evidence appearing real." However, to the mountainator the evidence is not false but true. Fear leads to panic. A prime example of mountainating is the hypochondriac. The hypochondriac takes every minor ailment he or she has and exaggerates it until he or she is convinced it is a symptom of a major illness. Doctors offices are filled with mountainators.

A second destructive consequence of mountainating is in relation to time. Whenever problems occur the man-made mountain looms so large and overwhelming that the mountainator believes it will last forever. Their belief is, "this too shall last."

How would you react if you believed you would have to endure a hardship indefinitely? Chances are you would soon lose your belief that events in your life would turn out for the best. In other words, you would lose hope.

The loss of hope is the proverbial "last straw" before depression. To the mountainator, "Life is not good!"

Destructive Framing Type #3
Musterbations

One of the more popular and discussion oriented segments of my workshops occur when I talk about musterbating...MUSTERBATING! Now, I've written it, let's discuss what it is. Musterbations are *habitual* thoughts (musts, shoulds, or have to's) that one relies on as guidelines for success in life.

If the "must" contributes to the successful completion of a problem or dilemma (e.g., in the US, you must drive on the right hand side of the road), then it is constructive. However, typically musterbating is destructive because it is based on unrealistic absolutes with justice as the primary consequence.

While there are as many ways to musterbate as there are musterbators, I have listed the top ten. As you read over this list, contemplate if you habitually engage in one or more of them.

The Top Ten Ways to Musterbate

---

1. I must be perfect.

2. You must be perfect.

3. I must be loved.

4. I must be in control.

5. Things must be orderly.

6. Things must be simple.

7. Things must not change.

8. We must see eye to eye on everything.

9. I must get everything I want easily.

10. I must be treated fairly.

To live by one or more of these "musts" creates the illusion that when they are attained then life will be good and success can be built. If you are one of those who believe this then you are doomed for failure primarily because you have set up unattainable expectations for yourself and others.

There are three primary destructive consequences associated with self-established rule(s). The first is anger and rage. A prime example can be found in the increasing incidences of "road rage." Many drivers and passengers in motor vehicles have been killed or hurt due to the violation of someone else's rules (musterbations) for the road.

The second destructive consequence of musterbating is the guilt associated with not living up to personal expectations of perfection. This is especially evident in the area of religious perfection. I would dare say that most believers (regardless of their faith) live under a cloud of "da" ("woulda," "coulda" or "shoulda"). Instead of forgiving themselves for their "da's," they are punishing themselves with guilt and despair. As a result, their witness is not as strong as it could be without such guilt. They need to change their "da" to "do."

The third destructive consequence of musterbating is inflexibility. Musterbators cannot allow themselves or others to mentally or physically bend to the circumstances and simultaneously maintain self-control and composure. As such, logic and reason is difficult to obtain.

To the musterbator, "Life is bad!"

M$_3$

Each framing type was presented separately. This was done for two reasons. The first reason was so they could be more easily identified in your life with the second reason being to pointedly express the destructive power they will have. However, in the real world seldom are such delineations cut and dried. More to the point, framing types tend to occur in combination. For example, self-mutilators may also tend to exaggerate the severity of a hardship, thus further underestimating their ability to successfully cope with it.

THE HUMOR OF DESTRUCTIVE FRAMING

While the results of destructive thinking can be devastating, there are also humorous examples. Some of the more humorous examples can be found in some of the laws in this country. Typically, "crazy" laws are legislated as a knee-jerk response to an atypical event in hopes of deterring it from occurring again. Author Dick Hyman has written several books (e.g., *More Crazy Laws*) exposing some of the crazier laws. As you read some of the laws Hyman cites, try to imagine what the lawmakers were thinking when they passed them.

- in Barker, New Jersey, it is illegal to knock on doors or ring doorbells

- in White Cloud, Kansas, it is illegal to break out of jail

- in Prichard, Alabama, every man must wear a top to his bathing suit

- in Moscow, Idaho, it is illegal to hypnotize anyone

- in Boston, Massachusetts, it is illegal to own a dog more than ten inches tall

LIFE HAPPENS

Several years ago Hurricane Hugo paid an unwelcome visit to my hometown. Many homes were damaged or destroyed. The destruction was widespread despite every builders' intention to construct homes made to withstand environmental elements. The point is this, despite preparations to the contrary, circumstances can be devastating.

Likewise, no one is immune to the circumstances and challenges of life.

Life Happens!

When "life happens" we are called upon to choose how we are going to react. If we are destructive thinkers, then we have built our lives for failure and the circumstances will destroy us. "Life is NOT good!"

Does this lifestyle sound appealing? I hope not! Continue with me in the building process as we learn in Phase IV "how" to reframe your mental blueprint from destructive to constructive thoughts.

Success Point

TO BUILD FOR SUCCESS, FRAME YOUR MIND WITH CONSTRUCTIVE THOUGHTS

Phase IV
Plumbing For Success

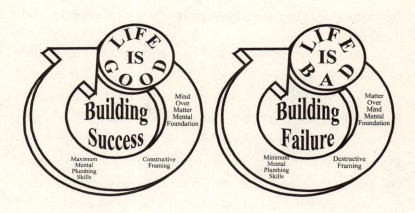

We learned from the last phase the critical importance that framing plays in home construction. It provides a support system for latter phases, as well as insulates and protects the inhabitants from potential detrimental elements.

Likewise, we learned that our minds have developed a mental frame, which contains thoughts that support our mental blueprints. If our thoughts are constructive, we succeed because despite any success roadblocks we know on a subconscious level that "Life is good!" Conversely, if our thoughts are destructive, we fail because success roadblocks affirm our belief that "Life is bad."

As mentioned in the last phase, "Life Happens," and roadblocks arise. When they do arise, all of us are prone to destructive thinking. Let's face it, it is easier to think destructively than constructively. Our ability to maintain a "Life is good!" blueprint is contingent on our mental plumbing system.

Mental Plumbing System

The fourth phase in the home building process involves the installation of the plumbing system. The plumbing system is a series of connected pipes that serve two purposes. One purpose is to carry water into the home to be used in various ways (e.g., bathing, cleaning, cooking, and drinking). Another purpose is to carry waste from the home. As a whole, the plumbing system cleanses, renews and refreshes the residents and their homes. I can't imagine a home without a plumbing system, can you?

Not unlike a home plumbing system, everyone has a mental plumbing system that is designed to cleanse, renew and refresh our minds of destructive waste; waste which constipates our minds. Why do you think they call it "stinkin' thinkin'?"

"Stinkin' thinkin'" is widespread in our society; if it wasn't, then more than two to five percent of humankind would be maximizing their potential. Many reach a point where they identify destructiveness in their lives but do not know how to maximize their mental plumbing skills for changing destructiveness to constructiveness. In other words, all the negativity and destructiveness of life goes in their minds with no method to flush it out. Interestingly enough, the problem lies NOT within the system (as everyone has one) but within the person's minimum use of the system because of a low IQ. To be more successful they need to increase their IQ!

INCREASE YOUR IQ

The letters "IQ," when written together are usually indicative of a person's intelligence quotient. To the layman, one's IQ is an innate measure of his/her success potential. It is widely believed that the higher the IQ, the more successful the person will become in life. A review of your high school annual will tell you this isn't so. In your annual you'll find that not all classmates with higher IQ's were successes in life *and* not all classmates with lower IQ's were failures in life.

Success came to both groups not because of an intelligence quotient but because of another type of IQ. An IQ more representative of one's success potential. The IQ I'm writing of is one's ability to Identify and Question destructive thoughts. We learned to identify destructive thoughts from the last phase. Identification is the first component needed to raise your IQ for more success.

In this phase, we will learn about the second component needed to raise your IQ for more success. The method from which this is accomplished is called the "IQ Method."

The IQ Method

1. Identify the Destructive Thought

Identification of destructive thinking is essential, for without it successful change is impossible! This is not as difficult as it seems. The rule for identification is this:

It's always a safe BET you are thinking destructively when your Behaviors (what you do), Emotions (what you feel) and Talk (what you say) are inconsistent with the reality of the situation.

Often times these are identifications you obtained after the fact. That's okay if you use these identifications to prevent similar inappropriate BET's in the future. The more you practice, the better you'll become.

2. Question It's Relevancy

With identification comes the second component of the IQ method; that being the questioning component. I have found that many people, rather than questioning the relevancy of their thoughts, tend to accept them unconditionally. They act and emote on those thoughts with a religious-like zeal. It's as if Moses came down from Mount Sinai with an eleventh commandment which says,

"Thou shalt believe everything thou thinkest!"

This commandment is adhered to by those with minimal mental plumbing skills. In their zeal, it never occurs to them that there could be alternative conclusions to negative circumstances. As such, they never develop the mental plumbing skills (aka questioning skills) needed to cleanse, renew and refresh their thinking. As a result, they build for failure.

On the other hand, those who build for success have maximized their mental plumbing system by increasing their skills in the art of questioning. They have become so skilled at this that whenever a challenge arises their mental plumbing system automatically "turns on" (much like one would turn a faucet to get water) to cleanse, renew and refresh their thinking.

The skilled use of questioning techniques to stimulate renewed and refreshed thinking is not new. For example, Socrates developed an entire teaching method based solely on the question and answer format. Specifically, Socrates would ask questions and his students would answer them. Of course most of us know this as the Socratic method.

Similar to the Socratic method, we are to be both the teacher and the student if we are to build for success. Whenever we "catch" ourselves acting, feeling or speaking (i.e., BET) in a manner inconsistent to a given situation, we are to immediately begin the questioning process. The answers we obtain will more accurately reflect the situation; thus, an immediate change in our behaviors, emotions and words.

The gamut of possible questions is endless since they must be specific to each situation. However, in order to assist you as you begin this method, I have provided sample questions:

If your initial conclusion is a mutilation (blame-related), ask yourself:

> "Why do I think I was the cause of the problem?"

> "Why do I think others are the cause of the problem?"

> "What else could have caused the problem?"

> "Does it matter who or what caused the problem?"

If your initial conclusion is a mountaination (severity-related), ask yourself:

> "Have I faced a similar crisis in the past?"

> "When the crisis was over was it as awful, terrible or catastrophic as I initially thought?"

> "Did I make a mountain out of a molehill?"

If your initial conclusion is a musterbation (justice-related), ask yourself the "WHY" question:

For example:

> Why must I be perfect?

Why must you be perfect?

Why must we all see eye to eye?

Why must I be loved?

THINKING FRAME SHIFTS

You'll probably discover that your initial attempts to raise your IQ will be difficult. This is to be expected. However, the more you practice identifying and questioning destructive thoughts the more your IQ will increase. A new you will begin to emerge as shifts in thinking frames enable you to build for success.

CONSTRUCTIVE FRAMING SHIFT #1
MUTILATIONS TO MENDATIONS

The first thinking frame shift which results from an increased IQ is in the area of blame. Instead of spending their time mutilating, menders spend it mending. Menders habitually question the relevancy of causality (e.g., self-blame, other-blame) when circumstances are difficult. They realize that to place blame for negative situations is a waste of time and not conducive to the success building process. In addition, they understand that many times challenges occur for a variety of reasons and rarely to a single cause. The mender's main objective is to look past blame in order to continue the success building process.

If we sincerely desire to build for success we must replace mutilating with mending. The more we do this the more our behaviors, emotions and words will push us to succeed! There are three primary benefits to mending.

The first benefit of mending is an improved self-image. Thoughts of optimism, positiveness and competence will abound. Like the childhood story about the little train which succeeded in climbing a steep mountain because it constantly repeated, "I think I can, I think I can, I think I can," so will you succeed when faced with mountain-size problems because you'll face them with an "I think I can, I think I can, I think I can" attitude.

A second benefit menders enjoy relates to how others begin to relate to them. Fortunately, menders are subject to the same self-fulfilling prophecy paradigm as mutilators but on the success side. For example, others relate to them in an optimistic, positive and competent manner because their self-image is such. The company and opinions of menders are sought out.

Not only will menders' company and opinions be sought out, but they seek out the company and opinion of others. They view their fellow man as optimistic, positive and competent. As such, they bring out the best in others. The ability to bring out the best in others is the third benefit of mending.

CONSTRUCTIVE FRAMING SHIFT #2
MOUNTAINATIONS TO MODERATIONS

The second thinking frame shift, which results from an increased IQ is in the area of severity. Instead of spending their time mountainating, moderators spend their time moderating. Moderators are not habitually prone to extremes. As such, you will not typically hear them awfulizing or terriblizing in reaction to negative circumstances. Through moderating, they seek and find middle ground.

Seeking middle ground also means they do not minimize the severity of a situation. Moderators realize there are times when circumstances are awful, terrible or catastrophic. However, this realization occurs ONLY after objective questioning, and after actions which failed to solve or manage the problem have occurred.

To build for success we must raise our IQ so that we replace mountainating thoughts with moderating thoughts! The more we do this, the more our behaviors, emotions and words lead us to more success. There are two benefits from moderating.

The first benefit of moderating is that faith replaces fear. Where once false evidence appeared real; *NOW* real evidence appears real. I guess you could say "REAR" (i.e., real evidence appearing real) has replaced "FEAR." To live without unrealistic fears means to live a life without panic and anxiety. Wouldn't a less stressful life be wonderful?

The second benefit of moderating lies in relation to time. Moderators stand back from the challenge of the moment and realize, "This too shall pass." My wife and I learned the power of this benefit during her pregnancy with our first child. As is the situation with many expectant mothers, during the first trimester my wife experienced daily bouts with morning sickness. One of my co-workers, upon hearing her sickness, calligraphed and framed my wife an affirmation that said, "This too shall pass." My co-worker's gift of kindness did not relieve the physical symptoms of my wife's morning sickness, but it was a source of inspiration and hope for her that a better day was coming. Both my wife and I have relied on this affirmation many times over the years when challenges occur. Just as it worked for us, it will work for you. The ability to see better times in the future is the substance of which faith, hope and optimism are developed.

Constructive Framing Shift #3
Musterbations to Mediations

The third thinking frame shift, which results from an increased IQ, is in the area of justice. Instead of spending their time musterbating, mediators spend it mediating. Mediators habitually question the necessity of absolutes (e.g., musts, shoulds, have tos) as guidelines for success in life. Thus, you will not typically hear them musterbating in reaction to negative circumstances.

To build for success we must (note: this is a rational must not a musterbation), overcome negative circumstances by replacing musterbations with mediations. Mediations are simple thoughts of desire, not absolutes. Following are the ten ways to mediate.

THE TOP TEN WAYS TO MEDIATE

1. I'll do the best I can.

2. You do the best you can.

3. If you don't love me I'll survive.

4. I can't control everything.

5. I can live with disorder.

6. I like for things to be simple but I can live with complex.

7. Change is the road to progress.

8. We can coexist even if we don't see eye to eye.

9. I am willing to work and sacrifice to get what I want.

10. An unfair world will not stop me.

To build for success we must raise our IQ so that we replace musterbating thoughts with mediating thoughts. The more we do this, the more our behaviors, emotions and words lead us to more success. There are two benefits from mediating.

The first benefit of mediating is that the chronic anger and guilt commonly associated with musterbating is lessened. No longer do the mediators live under a cloud of "da" (i.e., "woulda," "coulda," or "shoulda"). Instead of "da," they thrive in a sunny atmosphere of "do." Success building action is their focus.

A second benefit of mediating lies in an increase in mental flexibility. When negative circumstances arise, mediators are more capable of bending and rolling with the punches. They are the ones whose friends commonly refer to as "laid-back." Their mental flexibility allows them to maintain self-control and composure in potentially destructive situations.

It Works!

Aren't you excited? "The IQ Method" works! Just as surely as you can build a mental frame for failure, you can build a mental frame for success. Prosperity, peace of mind and physical health can be yours! However, the choice is up to you. Utilize your power of choice and practice, practice, practice; your IQ will increase in proportion.

GENERAL BENEFITS

I think you'll agree that the specific benefits discussed under each frame shift are tremendous. However, there are cumulative benefits from all three.

Benefit #1 Your Potential Will Maximize

The first cumulative benefit an increased IQ generates is in the maximization of your potential. A routine replacement of destructive thought frames with constructive thought frames produce a wonderful and powerful new you. You will reach new heights of success in any area you choose.

Benefit #2 You Will Be A Better Communicator

A second cumulative benefit an increased IQ generates lies in your ability to more effectively communicate with others. Those who are skilled at identifying and questioning their own destructive thoughts learn to identify them in others. However, it should be noted that it's not wise to identify their destructiveness; to do this might result in bodily harm to you! Rather, it would be more effective and conducive for effective communication to gently (and non-judgmentally) lead them through a series of questions designed to help THEM draw new conclusions. The ability to identify and question is a powerful communication tool.

Benefit #3 You Will Be More Marketable

The mending, moderating and mediating skills of an optimistic thinker are in high demand in the marketplace of life. Their skills are valued and they command top dollar as they utilize them in their professional lives. A high IQ enables them to meet and effectively handle the challenges of life.

Success Point

TO BUILD FOR SUCCESS, PLUMB (CLEANSE) YOUR MIND BY INCREASING YOUR IQ

Phase V
Electrifying For Success

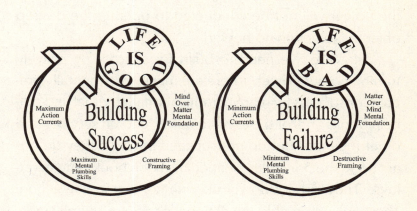

The plumbing phase in home building is essential in that it allows future inhabitants a method to cleanse, renew and refresh themselves and their home. Likewise, in order to build for success (i.e., prosperity, peace of mind, physical health), we need a method designed to help us maximize our mental plumbing skills. This method, called the "IQ Method," cleanses our minds of destructive thoughts by renewing and replacing them with constructive thoughts. This is the essence of Phase IV.

Electrical System

The fifth phase in the home building process involves the installation of the electrical system. The electrical system is a series of wires that conduct electricity from a central power-producing source to outlets, receptacles and various appliances of comfort within the home. With the "flip of a switch" or the "push of a button," electrical power is at our disposal. However, without action on our part, the power will not be conducted to operate the desired object. No action-no power!

Likewise, we need to build for success by actively turning on our power. There are many who mentally prepare for success by reading motivational, spiritual and self-help books and/or by going to rallies, church services and other meetings but do not succeed because they do not act upon the principles gleaned from the books and meetings. They did not power up with corresponding action. These folks resemble the fictional character of Pollyanna.

Pollyanna was the main character in a novel written in the early 1900's by Eleanor H. Porter. In the novel, Pollyanna was taught by her father to play the "glad game." The sole rule of the game was for Pollyanna to *habitually* find the positive side to any unpleasant or difficult situation. That would have been sound advice had her father taught her to follow up this mental exercise with corresponding action. However, because he didn't teach her to follow up her "game" with action, she was ill prepared to act in order to change the unpleasant situation.

There are many who, like Pollyanna, approach life's difficult situations by playing the "glad game." Corresponding action is the last thing on their minds. Instead, they are looking for that knight in shining armor, sweepstakes win, or divine intervention as a solution to difficult situations in their lives. When these events do not transpire, the gloss of the "glad game" tarnishes and they become entrenched in a "Life is bad" mental blueprint.

On the other hand, there are groups of people who combine their IQ with corresponding action. They eagerly engage in actions that promote the best possible outcome in their lives. Through action, they are connected to their power source; a power source which strengthens their "Life is good" mental blueprint.

The remainder of this phase is dedicated to the review of seven action currents which will enable you to build for greater success. To facilitate recall, the seven action currents spell the word "CURRENT." By no means are these seven currents intended to be exhaustive of all currents; there are others, and I encourage you to make a list of them.

ACTION CURRENT #1
CONTRIBUTE

In my hometown there is an automobile dealer who has, over a fifteen-year period, increased the number of his automobile dealerships from one to six. His name is Ray McKenney. McKenney bought his first dealership during the economic recession of the early eighties. Against all economic odds, he built his dealership into a multimillion-dollar business. His rise to the top was rapid and lucrative.

Once I asked Ray to share with me the secret of his rapid rise to business success. Without hesitation, he replied, "Service." He further elaborated that from his first day in business his number one priority revolved around customer service. The ways and means to contribute to the customer's needs became an integral part of his staff's training. To this day, the attitudes and actions of his staff portray this philosophy.

However, emphasizing customer service is only a small part of the reason McKenney profited during the recession. Due to his modesty, he never mentions his personal service work. Ray is an active contributor. His contributions have included active roles in civic, church and youth-supported programs. He not only supports these programs with his money but with a more precious commodity, his time.

McKenney's willingness to contribute is not atypical or uncommon. Everyone who has built for success has done so partly because they have developed a lifestyle of contributing. Active contributors see a need and fill it. To them, giving is a way of life and not a sporadic activity.

The opportunities to give of yourself are everywhere. The only requirement that one needs is a willingness to give of one's time, talent and/or money. You'll find that once you begin to actively contribute, two benefits will transpire.

Contributing Benefit #1   You Help Others

The first, and most obvious benefit, is that you help others. There are many people in this world who, through no fault of their own (e.g., children, elderly), are in circumstances beyond their ability to overcome when left to their own devices. The factors stacked against them makes them powerless to change. In these situations *WE* need to be the change-agent. As change-agents, we could provide them with a hand-up not a hand-out.

The hand-up approach is based on the old saying, *"If I give you a fish you will eat for a day, BUT if I teach you to fish you will eat for a lifetime."* Active contributors teach others to fish, to read, to add, to believe in themselves, to accept challenges and many other things. Teaching others to fish results in a lifetime of self-sufficiency for the learner and a way to become a change-agent in their own lives.

No measure of giving is too little to make a difference in someone's life. Very similar to throwing a stone in a pond and watching the water ripple across the pond's surface, even a small contribution affects the person's entire life. Your giving changes the balance of the recipient's life.

Contributing Benefit #2   You'll Be Blessed

A second benefit of active contributing results in blessings to the giver. People who actively contribute are more blessed than those who do not! That's because giving automatically activates the law of sowing and reaping. The law of sowing and reaping is just as true and powerful as any other natural law. For instance, just as the law of gravity tells us that objects released will always fall to the ground, the law of sowing and reaping tells us that when you sow you'll always reap blessings. No exceptions!

Skeptical? Perhaps a simple illustration will decrease your skepticism. Think about the last time you smiled at someone. What was the outcome? If the person was like most, a smile was returned. In this brief scenario you sowed a smile...and you were directly blessed with a smile in return.

The law of sowing and reaping is really not as far-fetched as it seems. Isn't it human nature to respond in kind to someone? Knowing this, couldn't we be the one to activate the law by sowing positive and optimistic seeds into the lives of others? My challenge to you is to make it one of your daily goals to sow seeds of optimism into the lives of others. Try this for one week and see if you don't reap blessings.

Work the law and you will be blessed. Plant the seeds of contribution and watch them grow. The blessings that you receive from helping your fellow humans are innumerable.

In addition to direct blessings that you receive from helping others, contributing will also result in indirect blessings. Opportunities will come your way from unexpected and unanticipated sources. Much of Ray McKenney's business success came not from professional contributions but from personal contributions.

Is utilizing the law of sowing and reaping for financial gain wrong? This is a question that has spurred heated debate in my workshops. In one corner is a group arguing that when one sows to receive, then they are not giving from the heart. Therefore, since their giving is based on selfish motives, they do not deserve to profit.

In the other corner is a group who argue that it's OK to give and expect to receive. They further state that regardless of the giver's motive, the end justifies the means, as both the sower and the receiver have bettered their quality of life.

WHO'S RIGHT? That's a question you'll have to answer for yourself. Personally, I believe it is appropriate and useful to systematically utilize the law of sowing and reaping for financial gain if you sow with:

- a cheerful heart,

- a sincere desire to help others

- no expectation of receiving from the person or group to whom you contributed to

AND

- a purposeful continuation of the sowing and reaping cycle gathered from your blessings.

Let's be honest, money is important. It makes living easier. As such, if the law of sowing and reaping is there for our utilization...then utilize it...responsibly. Money makes living easier.

Contribute Now!

Action Current #2
Utilize the Power of Dreams

Art Linkletter tells an anecdote in his book, *Yes, You Can!,* of a drive to a piece of deserted property near Anaheim, California, with a man named Walt Disney. As the two walked the property, Disney began to paint a picture of a theme park that he wanted to build. He described in great detail the different "lands" such as "Fantasyland" and "Tomorrowland." During his description, Linkletter recalled thinking that Disney's dream was a fantasy which wouldn't appeal to people. The purpose of their visit was for Disney to give Linkletter an opportunity to buy the land surrounding his theme park. Linkletter could, in turn, sell it to developers who would build motels and restaurants on the property. Linkletter, not able to dream Disney's dreams, respectfully declined. Of course, all of us know that Disney went on to build Disneyland on the property. Linkletter estimates that he lost approximately one million dollars per step that day by not buying into Disney's dream.

Was Linkletter wrong? No. One person's dream is not another's. Everyone has to discover and develop his or her dream and not someone else's. I have studied the lives of successful people and have found that each of them had a dream they grasped and developed. Each of them however, most likely followed the same basic dream fulfillment steps.

Dream Fulfillment Step #1 Develop you dream pictorially

While cleaning out drawers, have you ever found an old photo album? What happened? Chances are you became lost in time as you began to look and reminisce over the pictures. Just as a camera is used to record pleasant memories, so do we need to develop a mental picture of a future event.

However, before you can develop a picture of a future event, you need to honestly answer the question, "What do I really want?" Many people want to be successful but have not determined "what" success is to them. You can not obtain what you do not see in your mind's eye. Everyone who has been successful in obtaining their dream began with the end in mind. This is not to say they knew every step that would be needed to get them there, it means they had a picture of the finished product ever before them.

Dream Fulfillment Step #2 Refine and Refocus your dream

Once you have developed the picture of your dream in your mind's eye, you need to refocus and refine the picture so that it becomes clear and well defined. This process is called imaging. You can create anything that you can imagine! If you imagine negative and bad consequences from life, then you will obtain them. Many times this is easier than the alternative, optimistic imaging.

Optimistic imaging is the conscious process of vividly picturing a desired dream in your mind until it sinks into the subconscious part of your mind thus producing results in the physical dimension. I first heard of the successful use of imaging in the late seventies. There was a basketball player at the University of North Carolina who, when he was going to shoot a free throw, imagined the basketball going through the net. Consequently, he led his conference in free throw completion percentage.

The ability to optimistically image is available to all. It is a learned skill! One way to learn this skill is to make a dream notebook. Browse through magazines, cut out and paste pictures which represent the fulfillment of your dream on pages in a notebook. At least once a day, look at the pictures in this notebook and imagine yourself as being in the picture and living the dream. This activity will not automatically fulfill the dream, BUT it will motivate you to persist until the dream is reached.

Dream Fulfillment Step #3 Energize With Enthusiasm

Enthusiasm is taken from the Greek word enthousiasmos which means, "having the God within." Perhaps this is apropos as the ability to reach seemingly impossible dreams goes beyond our capability. How can you be assured that your dream is worthy of enthusiasm?

Ask yourself:

1. Is my dream within moral limits?

2. Will the pursuit or fulfillment of my dream lead to a greater contribution to myself, family and/ or the world?

If you answered "yes" to both of these questions, then your dream is worthy of enthusiasm. You will not reach your dreams if you do not apply enthusiasm continuously throughout the process. Those who have developed, refocused and refined their dreams are some of the most enthusiastic and inspiring people I meet. Be careful not to ask them how they are doing if you do not really want to know. In their enthusiasm and excitement, they will tell you.

Dream Fulfillment Step #4 Affirm it

It's likely that most have used the expression, "Sticks and stones will break my bones but words can never hurt me." Is this true? If so, then why do we become emotionally distraught when criticism occurs? It's not true. Perhaps a truer statement would be, "Sticks and stones will break my bones but words can always hurt me." There is power in the words you say.

Thankfully, the power of the spoken word can also be positive and uplifting. The use of optimistic affirmations are necessary if you are to successfully reach your goals.

An affirmation is a brief statement or series of connected statements that reinforce your dream fulfillment.

Dream Fulfillment Step #5 Minimize Distractions

To reach your dreams, you must be able to minimize distractions. A distraction is anything that blocks you from fulfilling your dreams. In other words you need to FOCUS. Focus involves self-discipline. Early in the dream process you find that your dream will take priority in your life. It's as if every waking moment is spent in dream chasing. As a lifestyle, this is not healthy and is counter to true success (i.e., prosperity, peace of mind, physical health). Eventually you'll reach a point where you can begin to live a more rounded life. But there must be a span of time in which FOCUS is the order of the day.

Focus is proportionate to dream fulfillment. For instance, in counseling with teens, I always seek to detect whether they have constructive, active dreams in their lives. When they do, I immediately know they will tend to steer away from any distractions (e.g., drugs, alcohol, and sex) which could result in a derailment of their dreams. Likewise, to be successful we must minimize distractions in our lives.

DREAM

The five steps spell the word "DREAM."

D evelop your dream pictorially
R efine and Refocus your dream
E nergize with Enthusiasm
A ffirm it
M inimize Distractions

Do you think there would be a Disneyland if Walt Disney had not followed these steps? I don't think so, for it was Walt Disney who said, "If you can dream it you can do it, remember this whole thing was started by a mouse."

Likewise, if you follow these steps you will fulfill your dreams. Show me a person who can describe their dreams and I'll show you a person who is in charge of their life. At the end of each day ask yourself, "What have I done today to further my dream?" If you can answer the question by citing positive action, then you are on your way.

ACTION CURRENT #3
REMEMBER THE POWER OF PATIENCE

Some of my fondest memories of early childhood were the times I would sneak into my Dad's summer garden, pluck green beans off the vine and eat them. To this day, I prefer the taste of raw green beans to the taste of cooked ones. Not once during my childhood years did I ever consider the process my father followed which produced the beans. The product, not the process, was all that mattered to me.

However, as I grew older my natural curiosity wouldn't allow me to enjoy the product without knowing how the product came to be. In my quest for this knowledge, I began, as many success builders do, to observe an expert in the desired area of knowledge. In this case, unknown to him, I watched my Dad.

My Dad began the gardening process in the early spring. What followed seemed to me to be a mysterious rite (at least mysterious to an eight-year-old boy) which led to various kinds of produce, but more importantly to me, green beans.

The Mysterious Rite of Gardening

My Dad would begin the mysterious rite of gardening by preparing the soil for planting. Tilling the ground in straight and parallel lines was the first step. I always wondered why straight lines were better than circles or some other shapes. Once the rows were set, further soil preparation was done as he mixed several mysterious materials (e.g., manure) into the tilled ground.

With the soil properly prepared, and only the garden master knew when it was, each row was sectioned off. In each section seeds were planted which were to grow into the desired produce. Sometimes, I would walk with him in his garden and he would point out to me where the seeds for each crop were planted. He would talk as if he saw the crop sprawling over the ground producing luscious abundance. However, when I looked, I saw rows of dirt.

My inability to "see" in time beyond the rows of dirt lay in my limited knowledge of the law of gardening. However, my Dad, with his vast knowledge and experience, understood the law of gardening and looked beyond the rows of dirt to the end result.

The law of gardening simply states that between the time you plant a seed in the ground and it begins to grow above the ground, there is a period when nothing seems to be happening. Those unfamiliar with this law come to the conclusion that they had failed and wasted their time.

However, those familiar with the law of gardening, such as my Dad, knew they hadn't failed or wasted their time. They knew that rapid growth was taking place beneath the surface of the ground as the root system was preparing to sustain life to the forthcoming plant. Once the root system is developed, foliage will spring forth abundantly above the surface of the ground.

What do you think would have happened to my Dad's garden if he hadn't known this? He wouldn't have diligently worked watering, weeding and fertilizing the rows of dirt. Consequently, produce wouldn't have grown; more importantly, no beans! Fortunately, thanks to my Dad, there were always beans. My Dad was successful each year...his garden never failed to produce.

Little did I realize it at the time, but I had learned an important success action current from his gardening preparation and perseverance. Primarily, I learned the importance of combining optimistic thinking with active patience.

Active patience is the power twin of optimism. It is through the power of optimistic thinking that we open the door to the attainment of dreams in our lives. Once the door is open, and realities seem to overpower our dreams, it is essential to utilize the power of active patience to keep the door open. Without optimism and patience, all you'll get are rows of dirt; rows of dirt which don't produce beans.

There are three gardening tips which are essential for building active patience and, ultimately, success. They are tips which keep the door of optimism open when the entire world seems to be pushing to close it.

Gardening Tip #1 Prepare Your Soil

The first gardening tip is to utilize active patience in preparing your soil for success (prosperity, peace of mind, physical health). Successful soil preparation will cause the seeds you plant to develop a root system with branches that burrow deeply into areas of prosperity, peace of mind and physical health. The development of each branch is essential for lasting success.

There are many who spend their time pursuing their dream by developing one branch of the root (e.g., prosperity) while neglecting another branch (e.g., peace of mind). Once the dream is fulfilled and prosperity is reached, they do not have the necessary root system in place to support their new lifestyle. Lack of nourishment from an under-developed root system leads to foolish spending and bad habits. Instead of continued success, they are soon bankrupt and destitute.

On the other hand there are those, such as Michael Jordan, who, through active patience, prepared their soil for success. Along with developing the superior physical skills to play basketball, he simultaneously developed the mental skills necessary to fully enjoy the financial success he attained.

If asked, I'm sure Jordan would tell you that soil preparation, via active patience, is one of the reasons for his success. It will also be one of the reasons for your success. One of the quickest and easiest ways to prepare your soil is through motivational and inspirational resources (e.g., tapes, books, and meetings). These resources will renew and refresh your mind to the possibilities of dream fulfillment.

You may be thinking, "I've tried this and it doesn't work." If you are, then I strongly urge you to try it again...and again...and again! It's through repetition that you learn and incorporate success ideas into your life. I can honestly say there has never been a time when I didn't learn something new from rereading a book or listening again to a motivational tape. There are some that I repeatedly refer to (e.g., The Bible) for guidance and success principles.

Gardening Tip #2 Water, Weed, Fertilize

Soil preparation is essential, however, soil preparation without regular maintenance will cause success to be limited. Regular maintenance is the second gardening tip and it involves watering, weeding and fertilizing to be successful. While soil preparation focuses on indirect ways to support success, regular maintenance focuses on more direct ways to support success.

There have been many occasions in which people have shown extraordinary patience until the first signs of dream fulfillment begin to occur. Instead of continuing to exhibit the patience that got them to this point, they develop an "I want it now" attitude. In their haste, they engage in foolish actions that significantly reduce the full extent of their potential for success.

To fully maximize your potential for success, you must continue to water, weed and fertilize. This simply means that you resolve yourself to "do" something everyday, no matter how insignificant it may seem, which builds success.

Gardening Tip #3 Apply Thatch(er)

The third gardening tip for success is to utilize active patience by applying thatch(er) to your soil. This gardening tip was obtained from Margaret Thatcher, the former Prime Minister of Great Britain, who said, "I am extraordinarily patient provided I get my own way in the end." Need I write more?

ACTION CURRENT #4
REMOVE MENTAL BOUNDARIES

Several years ago one of my friends installed an underground fence system to contain his dog in a specified area. The way the system works is simple. The "fence" is actually a wire buried approximately a foot under the surface of the ground. The wire carries a mild electrical current that emits first a beeping sound and then a shock to the dog by way of its collar whenever the dog is within a few feet of the wire. The purpose of the beep is to warn the dog that a shock is coming if it doesn't move back from the boundary. After a few shocks, the dog learns to stay within the preset boundaries.

In my friend's case, the system worked wonderfully. My friend was happier because he no longer had to keep the dog caged in a dog lot, and the dog was happier with more space to roam. Then, disaster happened! My friend, forgetting the actual location of the underground wire, accidentally cut it in half while planting a shrub. The power source reinforcing the boundary was gone. Without a boundary, the dog was free to roam the neighborhood.

What do you think happened? Nothing. The dog remained in the preset physical boundary. Her mental boundary had become more powerful and restrictive than the unlimited physical boundary which now existed.

While dogs are not people, there is a powerful success analogy to be drawn here. Everyone, as a result of "shocks" in their lives, has limited their potential by restricting their mental boundaries. Boundary restricting begins in early childhood. For example, most four year olds would enthusiastically raise their hands to have the opportunity to sing; however, take that same group four years later and I dare say you'll find twenty percent of them as eager to show their singing talents off. In the intervening four years, their mental boundaries were restricted due to the "shocks" of life.

The "shocks" they received were probably to their self-images. A damaged self-image is the single most destructive result of a restricted boundary. From phase III we learned that the self-image is the mental picture we have of ourselves and of our ability to succeed. As such, it determines many aspects of our lives, such as the way we dress, our habits, our moral conduct, and our life mate.

Try as we may, we cannot hide our self-image. It is shown to the world through the choices we make. Choices which shout to the world our mental boundaries. Show me someone living below their potential level and I'll show you someone with a restrictive mental boundary. Likewise, show me someone maximizing their potential and I'll show you someone with a nonrestrictive mental boundary.

Is there hope for the restrictive?

Can our boundaries be stretched?

Can our self-image be changed?

Will our success rise in proportion?

Will it be easy?

The answer is "YES," to the first four questions and "NO," to the last one...but we can remove mental boundaries.

Mental Boundary Removal Technique #1 Increase Your IQ

The first technique for removing mental boundaries is to increase your IQ. We learned in Phase IV that a truer measure of one's success potential lies in their IQ; their ability to identify and question the truthfulness of destructive thoughts. Once identified and questioned, destructive thoughts are automatically replaced with constructive thoughts. Those with an unrestrictive mental boundary are successful in doing this. Their IQ's are high.

Conversely, those with a restrictive mental boundary have a low IQ. They are unable to identify and rid themselves of destructive thoughts. More specifically, they are psychological self-mutilators. Self-mutilators habitually and unrealistically take the blame for every problem in their lives. The more blame they take, the more restricted their boundaries become. The end result of a restricted boundary is low self-image and an inferiority complex.

The good news is that you can remove your mental boundary by increasing your IQ. The method, as explained in Phase IV, is easy and effective.

Mental Boundary Removal Technique #2 Develop Self-Discipline

The second technique for removing mental boundaries is through the development of more self-discipline. Self-discipline is simply the process of developing and attaining goals. Those who are undisciplined are not skilled at developing and attaining even the simplest goals. As such, their lives are chaotic. The more chaotic their lives become, the more it spins out of control. In order to psychologically protect themselves, they restrict their boundaries.

Stop the spinning by developing the habit of self-discipline. Develop this habit as you would any other habit...one small step at a time. Begin by setting a goal that is easily attainable in terms of difficulty and time. Once the goal is attained, you'll be motivated to set and achieve other goals. That's because you'll discover that when you do the things you need to do when you need to do them, you'll be able to do the things you want to do when you want to do them. That's empowering!

I have observed firsthand the empowering effects of this technique many times in counseling sessions with students. Often times, after only a few counseling sessions, students who have been taught to self-discipline themselves by setting and achieving small goals have made tremendous progress in removing their mental boundaries.

Mental Boundary Removal Technique #3 Free the Joneses'

The third boundary removal technique is related to the "keeping up with the Joneses'" syndrome. Those who spend their lives by "keeping up with the Joneses'" are consumed with comparing. Comparisons include professional status, material possessions, spouses, neighborhoods, schools and et cetera.

Constantly comparing yourself to the Joneses' will almost always lead to disastrous consequences. Disastrous in that comparisons lead to false conclusions of superiority or inferiority. Neither is conducive to success building.

Build for success and remove the mental boundary which comparisons produce by "freeing the Joneses." When you "free the Joneses" you deliberately refuse to compare any aspect of your life with someone else's.

From the first day I began the exciting field of success writing and speaking, I determined that I was going to "free the Joneses." I absolutely refused to compare my skills and talents with others in the field. I was not going to be intimidated by their gifts. Instead, I chose to learn as much as I could from them. Their teachings, combined with my experiences and training, have resulted in success for me. Likewise, regardless of the situation you are in, resist, with all your might, the temptation to compare. "FREE THE JONESES'!"

Mental Boundary Removal Technique #4 Daily Affirm A New You

The fourth technique useful for removing mental boundaries lies in monitoring the words you say. As previously mentioned, the words you speak are powerful. Their power lies in their predictive ability (self-fulfilling prophecy). If you constantly speak in terms of personal negativity and limitations, then your mental boundary is going to shrink.

An occasional self-effacing comment will not shrink you mental boundary. It's the cumulative effect of those comments that cause the shrinking. It would surprise most people as to the number of negative comments they make about themselves in one day. They tend to confuse self-effacing comments with humility. Do not be confused, they are not the same.

The answer to this dilemma is to replace self-effacing comments with self-empowering ones. Self-empowering affirmations are as powerful as self-effacing affirmations. Tap into this power by affirming a new you. Begin this technique by writing a commercial about yourself utilizing the following four steps:

a. make a list of the attributes, strengths and talents you currently possess

b. make a list of the attributes, strengths and talents you desire

c. combine these attributes, strengths and talents into narrative form (commercial)

d. every day for the next thirty days, whenever possible (twice per day minimum), enthusiastically read the commercial to yourself while gazing into a mirror

Will you feel silly? Yes, at first, but then you'll discover on the "nth" try (e.g., fifth, fiftieth, hundredth...), that you are believing what you are affirming. Belief leads to the removal of mental boundaries.

ACTION CURRENT #5
ENGAGE THE SUPPORT OF OTHERS

The fifth action current encourages us to engage the support of others. This concept is also known as "teamwork." Teamwork is an essential action current for everyone who truly wishes to build for success. Successful teamwork and cooperation is essential in literally every aspect of our lives. Positive and successful change will not occur without this action current.

In fact, this country was founded partly on this action current. When the Founding Fathers met in Philadelphia to finalize and sign the Declaration of Independence, some in the group were naturally hesitant to sign. Who wouldn't be? All knew the possible repercussions from such a gesture. It wasn't until Ben Franklin, that powerful motivator, said, "We must all hang together, otherwise we shall all hang separately," that everyone in the meeting was bold enough to ink their name to the document.

This is but one example of the importance that teamwork has in building for success. Allow me to use a contemporary historical example in which teamwork dictated success for one United States president and failure for another. During the Carter administration it was reported that Carter made many decisions without consulting advisors in that particular area of policy. He was the president, that was his prerogative. However, despite Carter's vast knowledge and training, some of his policies failed to work. As such, he lost the confidence of the voting population, thus losing his reelection bid to Ronald Reagan.

Conversely, Ronald Reagan was a president who depended heavily upon his advisors. Unlike Carter, Reagan utilized his knowledge, training and his *team* of advisors. While he had the final say in each policy decision, his opinion regarding a policy was not so strong that it couldn't be changed. Reagan's reliance on his team led to many successful policies. I dare write that Reagan's presidency was one of the most popular of all presidencies among the constituents in United States history.

These are but two examples of the power that teamwork can have in building success. Without teamwork the individual's mind is left to feed upon itself. Anyone's mind, which feeds upon itself, will soon become malnourished. Avoid mental malnourishment by engaging the support of others. It's true that two heads are better than one; it's truer that four heads are better than two (but only when the four heads are working together to achieve a common goal).

As such, it is imperative to build a team capable of working to achieve the successful completion of a goal. There are five team-building components, which form the core of all successful groups.

Team Building Component #1 Choose Your Team Members Wisely

The first component to consider when developing a team lies in the wise selection of team members. Select members whose mental blueprints shout to the world, "Life is good!" Studies have shown that it takes three optimistic people to change the thinking of one pessimistic person. Any number less than that, and the gloom and doom of the negative person overtakes the entire group. If only one pessimistic person can make that much of a difference, what do you think two or more pessimistic group members can do to a group?

Of course, experience probably has already answered that question for you. Most optimistic people can relate an experience in which they served on a committee in which there was one or more pessimistic members. It wasn't a pleasant experience, was it? One bad apple did spoil the whole bunch. All of these heartaches and frustrations could have been avoided had you chosen your team members wisely.

Team Building Component #2 Learn to Resolve Conflict

Let's assume that you've chosen your team members wisely. All members are optimistic, bright and positive. No pessimism equals no conflicts...goal completion, here you come. Right? Wrong! Regardless of the optimistic mental blueprints of the team members, the potential for conflict is there. That's because each member views the goal's solution based on his or her funneling experiences. As such, they don't always see the solution in the same way as fellow members. When this occurs, conflict develops.

However, unlike the group with pessimistic members, optimistic members are skilled at resolving a conflict when it arises. Together they develop a mutual solution to the conflict by creating a "win-win" situation. A "win-win" situation happens when members view conflict not as an obstacle but as an opportunity to utilize each other's experience to complete a common goal.

Team Building Component #3 Make Every Member Feel Important

The third team building component taps into the most fundamental psychological need of every human; that is the need to feel important. Everything you do, everything I do, everything everyone does is motivated by feelings of importance. Generally this need is fulfilled when others appreciate you or when others show you appreciation.

Think for a minute about the last time someone expressed appreciation to you for a job well done. How did you respond? You felt important and probably worked even harder in order to sustain their appreciation.

In all walks of life it is essential to fulfill another's need to feel important by expressing appreciation toward them. In no other situation is this more true than within your team. Team members who are skilled at fulfilling another's need to feel important generally are the most persuasive and popular of all team members.

One note of caution, appreciation must be sincere. Insincerity and bribery will not work because most people see through this as easily as they see through a glass window. Just as a glass window can be easily broken, so too will the influence and trust that you desire from teammates be broken if you pass out insincere appreciation.

Team Building Component #4 Develop A Listening Attitude

The fourth component in building a successful team is the skill of listening. The ability to listen to another, through the words they say, their facial gestures and their body language, is the most difficult of all skills. That's because we weren't taught to do it. Instead, we were taught to so enjoy the sound of our own voices that we are simply waiting for another to stop talking in order to have our say. This is called the "shut-up and let me talk" attitude.

This attitude is not conducive to successful communication within the team atmosphere. Replace the "shut-up and let me talk" attitude with a listening attitude. A listening attitude begins and ends with giving someone else your undivided attention. It conveys to the person that what he or she has to share is important and that his or her opinion matters.

Do you want to leave lasting impressions on your teammates? Then develop a listening attitude, it's the most sincere form of flattery that one person can give to another.

Team Building Component #5 Do Unto Others

The last component needed to build and maintain effective teamwork comes from the best book ever written, the *Bible*. In the *Bible*, Jesus tells his disciples that "...in everything, do to others what you would have them do to you..." (Matthew 7:12-NIV) In other words, follow the golden rule.

Action Current #6
Now Is The Time

One of the more popular television programs from the fifties was "The Millionaire." Each week, the main character, Michael B. Anthony, through an anonymous benefactor, gave some lucky and unsuspecting person a check for one million dollars. The only catch was that the recipient couldn't tell anyone where the money came from, or it would be immediately returned to the benefactor.

Let's pretend that a spin-off from the program aired today. Instead of calling it "The Millionaire," it's called "The Pennyaire." Guess who the unwitting recipient is? That's right, you! In this program, Michael B. Anthony appears to you with an offer you find irresistible. He has offered to give you 86,400 pennies each day for the rest of your life to spend as you wish.

However, to add drama to our show there is to be a catch. The catch is that you must spend the entire amount on yourself each and every day. You can't invest it for later use, and you can't give it away. It must be used by you each day or you'll lose it forever.

"No problem," you say, "I can easily do that." Can you? I'm sure that the first few weeks or months you will eagerly spend every penny every day. However, soon the time will arrive when you'll become blasé about the money and live entire days without spending some or all of it. What was once a powerful motivator to you is now being taken for granted...after all, you reason, I'll get more tomorrow.

In actuality, everyone is given something more valuable than pennies each day; that being, *time*. Instead of 86,400 pennies per day we are given 86,400 seconds each day. The way and manner we spend it is our choice. However, any time not spent in the pursuit of prosperity, peace of mind and physical health (i.e., success) is wasted through procrastination.

Procrastination is the number one killer of success. The temptation to procrastinate occurs in every setting.

The following example of procrastination from the sales field was shared with me by Mack Petrea of Textilease Incorporated.

1. 8:00-10:00...arrive at work, check messages, drink coffee, talk to other sales representatives, check over proposals

2. 10:00-10:45...make first cold call

3. 10:45-11:00...getting close to lunch...nobody will see me now

4. 11:00-12:30...go to lunch

5. 12:30-1:30...too soon after lunch...nobody will see me now...check messages, paper work, talk with other sales representatives

6. 1:30-2:30...make second cold call

7. 2:45-3:30...too hot outside...stop and get ice cream, walk in mall

8. 3:30-4:00...too late in the afternoon...no one will see me now

9. 4:00-5:00...go back to office, check messages, talk with other sales representatives, go home

This scenario, while perhaps extreme, is representative of many people. Many unwittingly build for failure by allowing procrastination to consume their 86,400 seconds.

Do you procrastinate? You do if you *habitually* put off chores which could build for success. Not only will the chore go undone, but a high level of anxiety will overtake you as the deadline approaches.

If undone chores lead to high anxiety, then why procrastinate? The answer is obvious, it's more rewarding to put off an unpleasant chore than to complete it and reap the benefits.

In other words, it's easier to maintain failure than to obtain success by overcoming procrastination; that is until the anxiety associated with the failure becomes unbearable. Then, and only then, will we act. Unfortunately, action at this point is usually too late...the window for opportunity has closed. Once that happens, it's impossible to go back and reclaim those wasted moments and opportunities.

While you can't go back and reclaim those wasted moments and opportunities, you can create new moments and opportunities. To do this you have to overcome procrastination. The most effective way to do this is to develop a "Now is the Time" philosophy of life. Don't put it off, act now! There are two actions which will help plug you into a "now is the time" philosophy of life.

Action #1 Start Small

The first action essential to overcoming procrastination is to make a "to do" list. From the "to do" list, choose a neglected chore and complete it. You'll find that doing the easy chore is so empowering and motivating that you'll look forward to completing the others.

With repetition, completing chores becomes habitual. Habitual in that you will automatically set "to do" lists and them complete the items on them. Within a short time, you will forget that you were ever a procrastinator.

Action #2 No Time Excuses

A second action essential to overcoming procrastination is to ban the "I don't have time" excuse forever. My typical response when I hear someone say this is, "Bull!" The time they have is no more or less than others. Where would this world be today if Thomas Edison, Martin Luther King, Albert Einstein, Benjamin Franklin, Jonas Salk, Madame Curie, Jesus Christ and many others would have said, "I don't have the time."? Model from them, make the time.

Make the time to pursue a healthy balance of prosperity, peace of mind and physical health. Make the time to embrace those people (e.g., family, friends) and activities (e.g., watching sunsets, reading, socializing, laughing, hobbies) that you hold near and dear. Enjoy the moment NOW! If you don't, your golden years will be filled with "woulda's" and "shoulda's." Remember:

Yesterday is a canceled check.

Tomorrow is a promissory note.

Today is the only check you have.

Spend it wisely...those 86,400 seconds pass quickly.

ACTION CURRENT #7
TAKE CARE OF THE SPIRIT

Within every person's body lives their spirit. Our spirit is the core of our existence as it is the life-giving force within us. The Christian believes this spirit to be the Holy Spirit of God living within them. Whether Christian or not, our spirit determines the degree of efficiency to which our body and soul operates. A healthy spirit leads to enthusiasm and success, and a sick spirit leads to apathy and failure.

The key to a healthy spirit lies in prevention. There are three preventive techniques necessary for taking care of the spirit.

Preventive Technique #1 Develop a Sense of Humor

One of my colleagues in the educational profession has a message on his personal voice mail, which says:

> "Hello, Welcome to the psychiatric hotline. If you're obsessive-compulsive, press one repeatedly. If you're co-dependent, please ask someone to press two. If you're multiple personality, please press three, four, five and six. If you're paranoid-delusional we know where you are and what you want...just stay on the line so we can trace the call. If you're schizophrenic listen carefully and a little voice will tell you which number to press. If you're depressive, touch any key, no one will answer."

This message is not intended to belittle those who battle mental illnesses, its primary intention is to provide humor to the caller. Humor, and its byproduct laughter, are valuable techniques for taking care of the spirit. Psychologist Laurence J. Peter, in his book *The Laughter Prescription*, has listed at least five benefits which can be attributed to humor and laughter. According to Peter, humor:

1. gives immediate relief from emotional stress

2. keeps aches and pains from intensifying because it temporarily takes the person's mind off the pain

3. stimulates the cardiovascular system

4. promotes healing

5. causes the brain to produce endorphins, a neurotransmitter, that acts as a natural opiate in the body

In addition to these five benefits, the person with a well-developed sense of humor is also more charismatic. As such, they are more appealing and attractive to males and females alike. Someone who can evoke laughter and humor into everyday life will brighten the day for those around him. They build for success.

A good example of the power of humor to evoke charisma can be found in the 1996 presidential campaign.

During this campaign, Bill Clinton effectively used his sense of humor to convey to the American people his human side. Conversely, his opponent, Bob Dole did not effectively use his sense of humor in conveying his human side to the American public. As a result, Clinton won reelection as president of the United States. Ironically, in the months following the election, Dole's natural humor surfaced in commercials and television appearances. Had Dole done this sooner, perhaps the election would have been closer.

Preventive Technique #2 Develop A Prayer Life

Joe Frazier, the former heavyweight boxing champion of the world, once said, "As important as roadwork is prayer." This is quite a statement of the importance of prayer considering the countless hours Frazier spent training his body for one forty-five minute boxing match. Frazier utilized the power of prayer to fortify his spirit and prepare him for the match.

Another who believed in the power of prayer as a spirit enhancer was the late Dr. Norman Vincent Peale. Peale, in his book, *The Power of Positive Thinking,* wrote, "prayer driven deeply into the subconscious can remake you. It releases and keeps power flowing freely."

Prayer is powerful! It keeps the communication lines with God open. With God, that's the key, true prayer is a personal give and take exchange with God...not just a give and not just a take. When prayer is used in this manner, it is a powerful problem-solving tool. Answers and insights will come to you when you least expect it.

However, answers and insights will not come if you do not pray. If you have not already established a prayer life, start one today. One method I recommend is the ACTS method. "ACTS" stands for the four essential components of prayer "adoration," "confession," "thanksgiving" and "supplication."

To incorporate the ACTS method, begin by setting aside one percent of each day (14 minutes) dedicated to prayer. It is helpful to pick the same time each day in a place where you will not be interrupted. Begin the prayer VERBALLY with adoration and praise, proceed to confession, followed by genuine and sincere thanksgiving to Him for His blessings, then as you feel led, share your difficulties (supplications) with Him while simultaneously affirming the desired outcome for each difficulty. Ask for His guidance and LISTEN to His reply.

Praying is highly therapeutic as it keeps you tuned in to God. Prayers are highly encouraging and comforting during the challenging times. They also fill you with thankfulness during the victorious times. Life is short. Pray hard!

Preventive Technique #3 Develop a Spiritual Tan

Each summer, thousands flock to the beaches, lakes, pools, backyards and so on with one goal in mind; to take most of their clothes off, expose their bodies to the sun and get a tan. "Sun worshipers" believe in the sun's power to tan, and the sun doesn't let them down. They simply relax and allow the sun to do its job.

Just as the sun has its job to do, so does God have His job to do. God's job is to figuratively give us a spiritual tan by enveloping us in His love and grace. Love and grace which can't be worked for but have to be accepted by His followers. Once accepted, He will never let us down. All we have to do is simply relax and allow Him to do His job. Unlike with the sun, we won't get burned!

Currents to Success

The people who have positively influenced my life were not only optimistic but bolstered their optimism with these seven action currents. The action currents are intricately woven throughout their lives. A prime example is a man named Archie Austin. I wrote about Archie in my last book entitled, *Optimistic Thinking: The Key to Success,* however, his story is well worth repeating. Archie is a successful businessman who has owned and operated an automobile body shop for many years. He once told me that he started the body shop in a garage in his back yard. He built his business by offering his customers' quality and service. Within a few years, his business had grown to the point that the back yard garage was too small to accommodate his customers' needs. He expanded the business by relocating to a larger facility. Archie is a success. He is a success in his personal and professional life.

What is the secret of his success?

The answer is simple. Archie is an optimistic thinker who built his success by:

- contributing freely of his time, talent and money

- utilizing the power of dreams to build his business into a success

- remembering the power of patience

- removing mental boundaries which may have limited his success

- engaging the support of his family and friends

- developing a "now is the time" philosophy

- taking care of his spirit

The world is full of "Archies." People who have built their character and wisdom and success through optimism, faith and action. It is my wish that every person has at least one "Archie" to emulate in his or her lifetime. If you have, you have been blessed. If you haven't, you need to find one. Maybe you are an "Archie" yourself. Maybe you can serve as a role model for someone else. This status is earned and not given to you. Use your earned status and contribute. The world appreciates you whether you realize it or not.

IN LIFE

To help you remember the seven action currents, I have put them in a poem entitled, *In Life.*

IN LIFE

In life, there will always be many paths to follow;

May you always choose the path that leads to health, happiness and prosperity

The one that is the result of expecting life's best regardless of the circumstances

Bolster your life by:

* giving a part of yourself to this world...the part returned will be much greater

* never forgetting the power of dreams...as long as you pursue your dreams you will always have hope and a sense of purpose

* remembering the power of patience

* believing in yourself...then your limitations will be nonexistent

* remembering the advice and counsel of others...even Jesus called the twelve

- not putting off any task, whether easy or difficult...you will conquer the great crippler of success—procrastination

- taking time to pray, laugh and love each day

Do these things and unlimited success will be yours...you will reach the end of life's journey prosperous and healthy.

Success Point

TO BUILD FOR SUCCESS, ELECTRIFY YOUR LIFE WITH
ACTION

PHASE VI
MAINTAINING YOUR SUCCESS

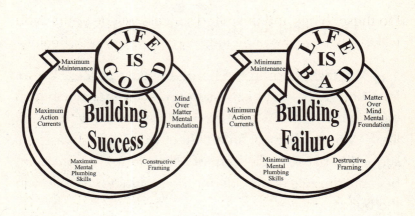

Congratulations, your dream home is complete! Every cent of the million-dollar sweepstakes money has been wisely spent to ensure quality, durability and character. These attributes were not accomplished haphazardly. On the contrary, they were accomplished by deliberate planning and effort during each phase of the building process.

Just as deliberate planning and effort is needed to build a home, deliberate planning and effort is needed to build success. Anyone, I repeat anyone, can build for success; they can obtain the delicate balance between prosperity, peace of mind and physical health.

Once the delicate balance of prosperity, peace of mind and physical health is achieved, what next? Next is the lifelong chore of maintaining success. We've worked too hard to lose it through lack of maintenance. Let's quickly review what we've worked to learn and build.

Phase I:
Developing A Blueprint For Success

The first phase in the home building process began long before the first nail was pounded. It actually began with your vision of what the completed home would look like. With the help of an architect, your vision was transcribed to paper in the form of a blueprint. The blueprint became the rule and guide for the contractor to follow in the building process.

Just as blueprints are utilized to successfully build a home, so are mental blueprints needed to successfully build a person. Due to a variety of influences, some positive, some negative, everyone's blueprint differs. The more one's blueprint *habitually* reflects a "Life is good!" mentality, the more success one will build. Challenges will be faced with optimism and action.

Conversely, the more one's blueprint *habitually* reflects a "Life is bad!" mentality, the more one will build for failure. Challenges will be met with pessimism and inaction.

If you are a pessimist, you need not despair, all is not lost! You, too, can build for success. That's because your mental blueprint is learned; anything learned can be replaced with new learning. You can literally rewrite your mental blueprint to build for more success.

Success Point #1: to build for success, develop a blueprint which shouts to the world, "LIFE IS GOOD!"

PHASE II:
LAYING A FOUNDATION FOR SUCCESS

The second phase in the home building process consisted of laying the foundation. When laying the foundation the builder digs and digs into the ground until he finds a rock-solid place to begin building.

Like the builder, if we are to build for success, we must dig and dig into our mental ground until we find a rock solid place. Optimistic thinkers have done this, thus laying a mental foundation that emphasizes "mind over matter." This foundation allows them to face challenges and problems by:

- focusing on their beliefs

- rising above the circumstances

- activating creativity

- reinforcing belief that "Life is good"

Conversely, the pessimistic thinker has not dug deep into their mental ground. As such, their mental foundation rests upon the sandy-shallow surface of "matter over mind." This foundation forces them to face challenges and problems by:

- focusing on circumstances

- sinking under the circumstances

- deactivating creativity

- reinforcing belief "Life is bad"

Success Point #2: to build for success, lay a foundation of "mind over matter"

Phase III:
Framing For Success

The third phase is the framing phase. The framing phase is the seemingly complicated chore of intricately joining a system of studs, floor joists and rafters to form the shell of the home. The shell serves as a support system for future phases and as protection and insulation to the home from external and internal elements.

Just as the framing system supports and protects the home, we must build a mental framing system which supports and protects our "life is good" mental blueprint. This happens as we become skilled in identifying the framing types which are destructive to our success. The three destructive framing types are mutilations, mountainations and musterbations. Essentially:

- mutilators face challenges by *habitually* blaming themselves or others

- mountainators face challenges by *habitually* exaggerating the severity of it

- musterbators face challenges by *habitually* relying on unrealistic absolutes (as opposed to desires)

Success Point #3: to build for success, frame your mind with constructive thoughts

PHASE IV:
PLUMBING FOR SUCCESS

The fourth phase in the home construction process involved the installation of the plumbing system. The plumbing system transports water to and from the home. Water is essential for quality of life as it is used to cleanse, renew and refresh the residents and their home.

Not unlike a home plumbing system, everyone has a mental plumbing system designed to cleanse, renew and refresh their minds of destructive waste. ANYONE can rid themselves of destructive waste by increasing their IQs. Our IQ is a measure of our ability to identify and question destructive thoughts. The higher our IQ, the more we will plumb our mind for more success by thinking constructively. The three constructive thinking frame types are mendations, moderations and mediations. Essentially:

- mendators face challenges by *habitually* seeking to mend

- moderators face challenges by *habitually* taking the middle ground

- mediators face challenges by *habitually* seeking desires (as opposed to unrealistic absolutes)

Success Point #4: to build for success, plumb (cleanse) your mind by increasing your IQ

Phase V: Electrifying For Success

The installation of the electrical system is the focus of phase five. The electrical system is a series of wires that conduct electricity from a power plant to the home. However, in order to make the system work, action is required...actions such as plugging in an appliance or turning on switches.

Likewise, we need to build for success by actively electrifying our lives with action. Action currents are essential for building success. In this book, you were given seven action currents that WILL lead you to a more successful life. They were the actions currents of:

- Contributing

- Utilizing the power of dreams

- Respecting the power of patience

- Removing mental boundaries

- developing a "Now is the time" philosophy

- Taking care of the spirit.

Success Point #5: to build for success, electrify your life with ACTION

MAINTENANCE

Home maintenance, sounds like fun doesn't it? In many homes across America home maintenance is also known as the "honey-do" list. Husbands, you know what I mean, that's the list your wife hands you with requests of "honey-do" this and "honey-do" that. While maintenance is not something your ordinarily want to do, it's something that is essential for the upkeep of the home. Lack of maintenance will result in deterioration both from elements within and without.

Scientists call this type of deterioration "weathering." It's an unavoidable and natural process of nature. As I polish us this last phase, it is Thanksgiving weekend and I am enjoying it with my family (on my wife's side) in a beautiful beach house. The house, only five years old, is showing signs of weathering. Without maintenance, the house will soon lose its luster and beauty. I'm sure that during the spring of next year the owners of the home will busily perform routine maintenance chores (e.g., painting and carpet cleaning).

What do you think would happen to the home if the owners decided not to fight the effects of weathering by performing routine maintenance? Within a few years, their beach home would likely become a money-pit, as extensive repairs would be needed to restore the house to its original mint condition. Constant maintenance is required!

The Big "C"

Constant maintenance is also required if one is continue to live successfully. A life without maintenance will result in the deterioration of the success that you have built. While this phenomenon is widespread, perhaps the most publicized examples are found in the world of sports. There are many professional sport teams who fail to repeat as champions primarily because they quit building upon the things that led to their championship success.

Instead of riding the big "C" of championship, soon they are succumbing to the big "C" of complacency. Complacency occurred because they felt too good about themselves and/or their accomplishments. They were content to enjoy the fruit of their labor as opposed to doing the things that were responsible for their success in the beginning. Their hunger was gone!

Complacency can happen to anyone at anytime. Whenever it does, the complacent individual (group, team, et cetera) makes a "U-turn" from prosperity, peace of mind and physical health. A prime example of complacency can be found in the last book of the *Bible*. In the book of Revelation, the Apostle John wrote a letter to the church of Laodicea about their complacent attitude toward the Christian faith. This particular church was started based on the fervent belief that the Christian gospel needed to be shared to as many people as possible. Despite negative circumstances (e.g., poverty, persecution), the church thrived. However, thriving led to complacency as fervency and hunger for sharing the gospel diminished. God, through the Apostle John, admonished them to rekindle the fire of faith or risk the consequences. This admonition came solely because they allowed the big "C" to overtake their lives. They rested on the fruits of their labors while simultaneously ceasing to spread the gospel.

The example of the Laodecian church does not mean that you shouldn't enjoy the fruits of your labor. You should, that's why you built success. What it means is to simultaneously enjoy *and* build for greater success. Anyone can avoid the big "C" if they learn their alphabet.

Alphabet...Affirm

The first letter you need to learn is the letter "A." "A" stands for affirm. Much has been written in this book about the power of verbal affirmations. That's because they work. Utilize their power to remind you of the success points presented in this book. At periodic times each day, repeat the following:

"To maintain success I will continue to:

* develop a blueprint which shouts to the world, 'Life is good!'

* lay a foundation of 'mind over matter'

* frame my mind with constructive thoughts

* plumb (cleanse) my mind by increasing my IQ

* electrify my life with ACTION

* replace complacency with constant mainte-nance

Alphabet...Belief

The second letter you need to learn is the letter "B." "B" stands for belief. Affirmations alone aren't enough. You have to believe what you're affirming. The key to believing what you are affirming lies in repetition. For example, the first time you affirm the success points, you may feel silly and doubt that affirmations work. It's possible that feelings of silliness and doubt linger through several hundred affirmations...but, eventually you'll begin to believe what you affirm. When this occurs, you'll proceed to the next letter in the alphabet.

Alphabet...Corresponding Action

Belief preceded by affirmations automatically leads to corresponding action. Try it, you'll see.

"LIFE IS GOOD!"

"Life is good," but it is not wonderful every day. This is an enduring fact that we must grasp. There will be days when challenges seem to surround and overtake us. Times when assaults are fast and furious. Yet, I have found that the consistent application of the six phases, even while in the midst of the challenge, is essential for my success. They should be essential for yours also.

If you will build your life based on the principles espoused in this book, you will achieve the total package of success. Instead of measuring success with prosperity, fame, or wealth, you will measure it with peace of mind, physical health and prosperity. Unlimited success will be yours.

SUCCESS POINT

TO BUILD FOR SUCCESS, REPLACE COMPLACENCY WITH CONSTANT MAINTENANCE

References & Recommended Readings

Anthony, R. *Doing What You Love, Loving What You Do.* Berkeley. NY. 1991.

The Bible.

Brooks, M. *Instant Rapport.* Warner Books. NY. 1989

Capps, C. *Faith and Confession.* Harrison House. OK. 1987.

Capps, C. *Success Motivation.* Harrison House. OK. 1982.

Dyer, W. *Your Erroneous Zones.* Avon Books. NY. 1977.

Fox, E. *Find and Use Your Inner Power.* Harper & Brothers. NY. 1937.

Glasser, W. *Taking Effective Control of Your Life.* Harper and Row. NY. 1984.

Hartness, J. & Eskelin, N. *The 24 Hour Turn-Around.* Revell. MI. 1995.

Hill, N. *Napoleon Hill's A Year of Growing Rich.* Penguin Books. USA. 1993.

Hill, N. *Think and Grow Rich.* Fawcett Crest. Greenwich CN. 1960.

Hyman, D. *More Crazy Laws.* Scholastic Inc. NY. 1992.

Linkletter, A. *Yes, You Can.* Sphire Books. NJ. 1982.

McCarter, R. *Optimistic Thinking.* Professional Press. NC. 1994.

McCarter, R. *Choose Life.* Interactive Resources. TN. 1994.

Mandino, O. *Og Mandino's Great Trilogy.* Fell Publishers. NY. 1981.

Peale, N. V. *Positive Imaging.* Fawcett Crest. NY. 1982.

Peale, N. V. *The Power of Positive Thinking.* Fawcett Crest. NY 1952.

Peter, L. J. & Dana, B. *The Laughter Prescription.* Ballantine Books. NY. 1982.

Robbins, A. *Awaken the Giant Within.* Fireside Books. NY. 1991.

Schindler, J. *How to Live 365 Days a Year.* Prentice-Hall. NY. 1954.

Schuller, R. *The Be-Happy Attitudes.* Bantam Books. NY. 1987.

Schwartz, D. *The Magic of Thinking Big.* Fireside Edition. NY. 1987.

Seligman, M. E. P. *Learned Optimism.* Knopf Publisher. NY. 1990.

Stone, W. C. *Success Through A Positive Mental Attitude.* Pocket. NY. 1960.

About
Rob McCarter, MS, NCC, LPC

Most of Rob's life has been dedicated to helping others find solutions to challenges. So, it's no surprise that his life's journey has led into the helping profession. Rob has earned a masters degree in psychology and is licensed psychotherapist. He utilizes his training and experience with others on both an individual and group basis.

On an individual basis he utilizes the techniques of traditional psychotherapy with neurolinguistic programming (NLP) to teach success management skills. Based on sessions with Rob at Carolinas Counseling and Consulting, clients have experienced success in the following areas:

- *Attention Difference (ADD) Management*
- *Sports Management (the mental game)*
- *Stress Management*
- *Chronic Pain Management*
- *Weight Management*
- *Anxiety Management*
- *Confidence Management*
- *Fear Management*

On a group basis Rob is a much sought-after speaker and trainer. Through his company, Life Enhancements, he blends within his presentations a successful mix of real-life solutions with humor.

Rob's desire to reach as many people as possible led him to write three books on the subject of success through optimism. The first one is entitled, Optimistic Thinking: The Key To Success, the second entitled, Life Is Good! and the third, People Skills.

Rob is a husband, parent, author, coach, teacher, and wonderful storyteller. An expert in the field of maximizing human potential and the role it plays in success, Rob would be happy to talk with you about your needs in helping you to maximize YOUR potential.

Contact Rob about maximizing your potential in either of the following ways:

Carolinas Counseling & Consulting, LLC
35 North Main Street
Belmont, NC 28012
704.825.9998

Life Enhancements
PO Box 363
Belmont, NC 28012
704.866.2725
Fax: 704.825.7735

Web Address: LifeEnhancementsInc.com
E-Mail: Rob@LifeEnhancementsInc.com